KENNETH C. DAVIS

ILLUSTRATED BY SERGIO MARTINEZ

DON'T KNOW MUCH ABOUT

Rosa Parks

HarperCollinsPublishers

Photo credits: Pages 79 and 107, AP/Wide World Photos. All other photographs courtesy of the Library of Congress.

We would like to thank Ludlow Music, Inc., for permission to print the excerpt from "We Shall Overcome" on page 68. Musical and lyrical adaptation by Zilphia Horton, Frank Hamilton, Guy Carawan, and Pete Seeger. Inspired by African American Gospel Singing, members of the Food & Tobacco Workers Union, Charleston, SC, and the southern Civil Rights Movement. © 1960 (renewed) and 1963 (renewed) Ludlow Music, Inc., New York, NY. International copyright secured. Made in U.S.A. All rights reserved including public performance for profit. Royalties derived from this composition are being contributed to the We Shall Overcome Fund and The Freedom Movement under the Trusteeship of the Writers. Used by permission.

This is a Don't Know Much About® book.
Don't Know Much About® is the trademark of Kenneth C. Davis.
Don't Know Much About® Rosa Parks
Copyright © 2005 by Kenneth C. Davis

www.harperchildrens.com

Library of Congress Cataloging-in-Publication Data
Davis, Kenneth C.
   Don't know much about Rosa Parks / Kenneth C. Davis ; illustrated by Sergio Martinez.
      p.   cm. — (Don't know much about)
   Includes bibliographical references and index.
   ISBN 0-06-028819-1 (lib. bdg.) — ISBN 0-06-442126-0 (pbk.)
   1. Parks, Rosa, 1913– —Juvenile literature. 2. African American women—Alabama—Montgomery—Biography—Juvenile literature. 3. African Americans—Alabama—Montgomery—Biography—Juvenile literature. 4. Civil rights workers—Alabama—Montgomery—Biography—Juvenile literature. 5. African Americans—Civil rights—Alabama—Montgomery—History—20th century—Juvenile literature. 6. Segregation in transportation—Alabama—Montgomery—History—20th century—Juvenile literature. 7. Montgomery (Ala.)—Race relations—Juvenile literature. 8. Montgomery (Ala.)—Biography—Juvenile literature. I. Martinez, Sergio, 1937– II. Title. III. Series.
F334.M753P3834 2005
323'.092—dc22   2004014426

Design by Charles Yuen
1 2 3 4 5 6 7 8 9 10
❖
First Edition

ACKNOWLEDGMENTS

An author's name goes on the cover of a book. But behind that book are a great many people who make it all happen. I would like to thank all the wonderful people at HarperCollins who helped make this book a reality, including Susan Katz, Kate Morgan Jackson, Barbara Lalicki, Martha Rago, Rosemary Brosnan, Amy Burton, Meredith Charpentier, Dana Hayward, Maggie Herold, Jeanne Hogle, Rachel Orr, Lorelei Russ, and Drew Willis. I would also like to thank David Black, Joy Tutela, and Alix Reid for their friendship, assistance, and great ideas. My wife, Joann, and my children, Jenny and Colin, are always a source of inspiration, joy, and support, and without them my work would not be possible.

I especially thank Georgette Norman, director of the Troy University Rosa Parks Museum in Montgomery, Alabama, for reviewing the manuscript and providing helpful insights; Sarah Thomson for researching the photos; Sergio Martinez for his striking illustrations; and Judy Levin for her unique contribution.

CONTENTS

Rosa Parks

"Please stay off of all buses Monday."

Those are not the most famous or inspirational words in American history. They certainly aren't as memorable as "All Men are Created Equal" or "I have a dream." But in many ways these seven words are just as important as anything that Thomas Jefferson or Martin Luther King Jr. ever said.

These were the words that spread through Montgomery, Alabama, the day after Rosa Parks was arrested. And what was her crime? She wouldn't give up her seat on a city bus when the white bus driver told her to move— just because she was black. What happened next in Montgomery would change America forever.

Who is Rosa Parks? And why does she matter? What was so important about one lady refusing to move from her seat? She wasn't a president, like Abraham Lincoln. Or a general, like George Washington. She didn't lead warriors in battle like Sitting Bull. She didn't invent a machine that changed lives, discover a cure for a disease, or explore new worlds. Rosa Parks did none of the things that the history books usually talk about. She was an *ordinary* person who did something *extraordinary*.

Now, getting arrested on a bus doesn't sound that special. But it was a brave thing for a black woman to do in Alabama in 1955. Up until the Civil Rights movement, which she helped to start, there were two Americas—one white and one black. There were many laws meant to keep white and black people separate. In some places black people could not drink from the same water fountains as whites. They had to ride in separate cars on trains and sit in a separate part of buses. These laws made African Americans second-class citizens with fewer rights and fewer opportunities to learn, work, and live. It wasn't fair and it wasn't just.

Imagine if someone told you that you couldn't sit at the lunch table because your eyes were blue. Or if you couldn't go to a certain school because your last name was Smith instead of Jones. Of course that wouldn't be right. It might be hard to imagine that life in America could be that way. But for millions of blacks, that's what life was like for a very long time.

Like all the Don't Know Much About® books, DON'T KNOW MUCH ABOUT® ROSA PARKS tells a true story by asking questions. Sometimes these questions don't have easy answers, but the answers reveal how Rosa Parks and many other brave people in the Civil Rights movement fought to make life in America fairer for everyone. Her story shows how one person can make a difference in the world. And that may be the most important part of the remarkable true story of Rosa Parks.

CHAPTER 1

A Good Little Girl

Tuskegee Institute in Tuskegee, Alabama

Where was Rosa Parks born?

Rosa Louise McCauley was born on February 4, 1913, in Tuskegee, Alabama, about forty-five miles east of Montgomery. Tuskegee was not a big place; about three thousand people lived there. But it was home to the Tuskegee Institute, a school begun in 1881 by the famous Booker T. Washington. Born a slave, Washington was an educator who taught that black people had to have respect for themselves and their work. Rosa's mother loved his teachings and raised Rosa to love them too.

Why was Rosa's mother special?

Rosa's mother, Leona Edwards McCauley, was a teacher before Rosa was born. She had taught in her hometown of Pine Level, Alabama, and then in Tuskegee. Leona McCauley was unusually well educated for a woman in those days. Not many Southern women had enough schooling to be teachers, and it was especially rare for black women. She had even been to college. Rosa's grandfather had said he wanted his daughters to be educated so they'd never have to clean houses for white people.

Rosa's father, James McCauley, was a carpenter. He built beautiful houses, Rosa said, but he often worked far from home and would be away for months at a time. Leona McCauley wanted her husband to get a job teaching at the Tuskegee Institute so that Rosa would be able to go to school there, but James McCauley thought he could make more money as a builder. It was a hard time for Rosa's mother. Alone with baby Rosa, who was often sick, she missed her husband and the challenge of teaching.

Why did Rosa's family leave Tuskegee?

When Rosa was two, her family moved in with her father's parents in Abbeville, Alabama. Rosa had to share a dirt-floored room with three cousins. For Rosa's mother, this was even worse than being alone with a sick baby. After a few months, she decided they should live with her own parents in Pine Level.

Rosa's Grandfather Sylvester and Grandma Rose owned a small farm and a better house in Pine Level. James McCauley lived with them between jobs until Rosa was two and a half. Then he left. He visited for a few days when Rosa was five and her little brother, Sylvester, was three. After that Rosa didn't see her father again until she was grown up.

Sometimes he wrote to his wife; sometimes he sent a tiny bit of money; but Rosa and her brother grew up without a father. It's one of the many difficult things in her life that she doesn't talk about.

Did anyone think that Rosa would grow up to be famous?

When she was young, Rosa often had a fever and a terribly sore throat from infected tonsils. (Infections could be more serious in those days, because there were no medicines to cure them.) One of Rosa's earliest memories is of Grandfather Sylvester taking her to the doctor when she was only two and a half years old. Years later Rosa still remembers the red velvet coat and bonnet she was wearing, and she

recalls that she didn't cry when the doctor looked down her throat. When her grandfather brought her home, he told Rosa's grandmother and mother how good she'd been, and Rosa was very proud.

Rosa liked being "a good little girl," even though kids sometimes would tease her about being so good and wearing clean little white gloves. So while it wasn't obvious that she'd be famous, it was clear what kind of person she was going to be: Even as a young girl, she cared about being properly dressed and well behaved.

Why was Rosa so close to her grandparents?

After Sylvester was born, Rosa's mother went back to teaching. The nearest job she could get was in Spring Hill, about eight miles away. Eight miles is a long way to go if you don't have a car or even a horse. So at the beginning of the school week, Grandfather Sylvester would take Rosa's mother to Spring Hill in a wagon pulled by a mule. She would stay there all week and come home for weekends.

Rosa liked being with her grandparents, but she missed her mother. One time when she was trying to protect her brother from a spanking, Rosa said, "Grandma, don't whip brother. He's just a little baby and he doesn't have no mama and no papa either." So she must have felt sometimes that *she* didn't have a mother or a father. She also says that protecting her brother may have been one of the ways she learned to protect herself.

Why did Rosa's grandfather hate white people?

Grandfather Sylvester was born a slave years before the Civil War began in 1861. His father was a white plantation owner. His mother was a slave who worked in the plantation house. As a little boy, Grandfather Sylvester was beaten and starved, and he never forgave white people for the way his owners had treated him. Grandfather Sylvester didn't even like it when Rosa and Sylvester played with the white children who lived on the Hudson plantation next door, even though Southern black and white children often played together.

Grandfather Sylvester also taught his daughters and grandchildren that they should never accept "bad treatment" from anyone. He never did. Grandfather Sylvester had very light skin and straight hair and would sometimes pretend to be white in front of strangers. He liked to do things black people weren't allowed to do, like shake a white man's hand. If the white man found out that he'd just shaken a black person's hand, he would be really embarrassed. It was one of Grandfather Sylvester's ways of getting a tiny bit even with the whites for all their bad treatment of black people for so many years.

Grandma Rose felt differently about white people. Her father was a white servant who worked on the Wright plantation, where her mother was a slave. After the Civil War, as a very young girl, she took care of the Wrights' baby girl and lived in their house. Grandma Rose was calm and loving. She wasn't angry at the world like Grandfather Sylvester was, but she was tough. If Grandma Rose told you to do something, you did it, or else she whipped your bottom.

Rosa's grandmother and mother taught Rosa that the way to succeed was to "respect yourself and live right." Living right meant following the teachings of the Bible and of Booker T. Washington. Rosa had to be clean, honest, polite, and respectful of other people. Her mother said she must not make the mistake of judging people by how much money they had. What mattered were people's hearts and their self-respect.

So Rosa was taught to be a perfect little lady, but she also learned the joys of a little rule breaking, if the rules were wrong.

THE WAR OVER SLAVERY

The Civil War (1861–1865) was a long, terrible war fought between the Union (mostly Northern states) and the Confederacy (mostly Southern states). There is nothing "civil" about a civil war. It means a war fought between people who live in the same country, and in the American Civil War, more than six hundred thousand soldiers and sailors died in the bloody fighting.

While there were many disagreements between the Union and Confederate sides, the main issue that led to the war was slavery. Some Northerners, called abolitionists, wanted an end to slavery, which was legal in the United States; others just wanted it to be limited to the states where it was already legal and not be allowed in new states that were being formed. But many Southerners argued that people in each state should get to decide whether or not slavery would be legal there.

In 1863 President Abraham Lincoln issued the Emancipation Proclamation, which freed all slaves living in Confederate states.

BOOKER TALIAFERRO WASHINGTON

Booker T. Washington

In the 1880s Booker T. Washington and his students had built the Tuskegee Institute brick by brick—and first they had to dig up the clay and learn how to make the bricks! He taught young black men and women to read and write, and to be well-trained carpenters, mechanics, nurses, and cooks. He also taught academic subjects such as algebra, and he brought George Washington Carver, who was one of the most famous scientists of the time, to Tuskegee.

But in his writing and in his famous speeches, Washington seemed to promise that black people would go on being the same faithful laborers and nannies that they had been when they were slaves. Booker T. Washington wanted real equality for African Americans, but he believed that it would take some time—maybe even generations. He believed that, first, ordinary black Southerners had to be able to do the jobs that were available to them, and they had to be able to do them well and proudly. As a young boy, he himself had gotten a scholarship to a school, the Hampton Institute in Virginia, because he did the best job of sweeping and dusting a room that the admissions officer had ever seen.

Booker T. Washington's teachings offered not just education, but dignity and pride and self-respect to people who were trying to just survive.

Since Rosa's family owned their own farm, were they rich?

Their eighteen acres would be a gigantic backyard, but the property was small for a farm, and there were only two old people and two small children to take care of it. The same mule that took Rosa's mother to school every week was also their "tractor," pulling a plow at planting time. Rosa's family always had enough to eat, but they never had much money—even for important things. Rosa's tonsils made her so sick that she didn't grow properly. Her little brother was bigger than she was. But Rosa's tonsils weren't removed until she was nine years old because it cost too much.

Still, the family knew they were lucky to own land and a house. Owning land was one of the greatest dreams free black people held after the Civil War. It meant they could work for themselves, not for someone else. Most people living in the South were farmers, and people—black and white—who didn't own land often became sharecroppers. They worked on a plantation owner's land in exchange for a small part (a "share") of the crops they grew. At the end of the harvest, sometimes the owner would say that the workers owed *him* money because he made them pay for seeds and fertilizer and tools. After the war, when many Southern plantation owners had to sell property, Grandma Rose's father bought twelve acres of the Wright plantation. The other six acres and the house were a gift made years later by the Wright child Grandma Rose had helped raise. So Rosa grew up on land that had been part of the plantation her great-grandparents worked on. They were the only black family in Pine Level that owned land.

What did Rosa have for dinner?

There were no supermarkets or fast food when Rosa was a girl. Rosa's family grew lots of vegetables and peach, apple, pecan, and walnut trees. They raised chickens, a few cows, and probably some pigs. Rosa's family could grow most of their own food and sell or

trade eggs, chickens, and calves for things they couldn't grow. They picked wild berries and plums to make jam. Sometimes Grandfather Sylvester and Grandma Rose would take their grandchildren fishing—especially since Rosa didn't mind putting the worms on everyone's hooks. As an older woman, Rosa became a vegetarian, but she grew up eating the food of a Southern farm child: more vegetables than meat, but also catfish, fried ham, rabbit, and fried chicken. For the winter they had home-canned foods such as meat, fruit, and vegetables boiled and preserved in jars. With their own farm and lots of hard work, they had a healthy diet.

One thing Rosa's family couldn't grow was clothes. They would buy cloth from one of the few stores in Pine Level, and Rosa's mother would sew clothes for them. That wasn't just because they were poor. When Rosa was a girl, many people still made their clothes at home. And having clean, proper clothes wasn't easy for a family that never had much money. Rosa was proud of her mother's good sewing and, later, was a professional tailor herself.

Did Rosa's family have a big electricity bill?

If you've ever seen the mammoth homes in *Gone with the Wind*, forget it. Many Southern houses, even plantation houses, were actually quite small. However, we don't know what Rosa's house really looked like. Rosa talks and writes often about ideas, but not often about her life. She never talks about the house in Pine Level, except to say that it had been the Wrights' house and that her grandparents moved there from their little log cabin. Rosa also says they ate off a table that her great-grandfather had made by hand. She's proud of that table.

Knowing how important Booker T. Washington's teachings were to the family, we can imagine that Rosa's house was always neat and clean. But Rosa couldn't exactly hop in the shower, throw her clothes in a washing machine, or turn on a vacuum cleaner. Almost no farms or plantations had electricity, running water, or indoor bathrooms in the 1910s and 1920s, although some houses in towns and cities did. A wood-burning stove heated the house, which means someone had to chop wood. Water was drawn or pumped from a well. Rosa's family wouldn't have needed money for electricity, oil heating, or water bills.

❝I never see a filthy yard that I do not want to clean it . . . or a button off one's clothes, or a grease-spot on them or on a floor, that I do not want to call attention to it. **❞**

—**Booker T. Washington**, *Up from Slavery*, 1901

Why did Rosa love going to church?

All her life Rosa was proud to belong to the African Methodist Episcopal Church, called the A.M.E. It had been founded in Philadelphia in 1816 by Bishop Richard Allen. He had been a slave, and from the time he founded his church, he fought for abolition. People called the A.M.E. "the Freedom Church."

Rosa was baptized when she was two, and she loved church right from the start. She liked dressing up, seeing people, and hearing the hymns, prayers, and sermons. When she was sick or when white kids were mean to her, she would think of the hymns and psalms she had learned in church and from her grandmother. They made Rosa feel safe, strong, and protected. They made her feel brave. And along with the teachings of the church and of her family, they made her think a great deal about right and wrong.

AMERICAN VOICES

❝O freedom

O freedom

O freedom over me

And before I'd be a slave

I'd be buried in my grave

And go home to my Lord and be free. ❞

—From the spiritual "O Freedom," written by **Sarah Hannah Sheppard**
This is one of the songs Rosa Parks grew up with.

Slow, Southern Life

As Rosa was growing up, the world was changing fast. In 1910 the sixty-story Woolworth Building was being built in New York City. (For the next twenty years, it would be the tallest building in the world.) And in 1917, the United States joined the fight in World War I.

But change came slowly to tiny Southern farming towns. People in Pine Level were still living in the "olden days." In 1914 Henry Ford built the first modern assembly line for his Model T cars, and cheap cars became available for the first time. But when black people in Pine Level wanted to travel the thirty miles to Montgomery, they paid to ride with the one black man in town who had a car, and it had a top speed of about twenty-five miles per hour.

There were no telephones, or even radios, on Southern farms. "Victrolas"—wind-up record players—were popular, but Rosa's family never had one. Silent movies were all the rage, but Rosa never saw any. Kids usually played hide-and-seek, went fishing, explored the woods, and picked wildflowers. They played ball—when anyone had a ball—and Rosa distinguished herself as a really terrible ballplayer. Little girls played "ring games" like "Ring Around the Rosie," always wore dresses, sewed, and minded their manners. They also worked.

When did Rosa have her first job?

She did chores on her family's farm—all farm children did—but her first work for pay was picking cotton at the Hudson plantation when she was six or seven years old. Her family worked there because they needed extra money. Rosa says they worked "from can to can't"—from sunup, when you "can" see, to sundown, when you "can't" see. Slaves had said this same thing.

Rosa says that the children would make a game of it, trying to see who could pick the most, but it wasn't fun. Children were beaten if they got blood on the cotton, which was easy to do because cotton bolls are so sharp. When they couldn't stand up anymore because their backs and blistered feet hurt, they would work crawling on their hands and knees. Rosa never complained about hard work and, luckily, her health was better in the summer than in the winter. But she does say she admired one black man, Gus Vaughn, who wouldn't work in the fields or be polite to the overseer. Like her grandfather, Rosa liked to see people stand up for themselves.

Where was Rosa's first school?

Rosa attended the same one-room wooden schoolhouse in Pine Level that her mother had attended—and even had the same teacher. About fifty or sixty kids went there, from first graders to sixth graders. Rosa was good at her schoolwork. She had learned to read and count when she was three or four, and she loved reading, especially fairy tales.

Rosa liked her teacher and she liked school, but didn't think it was fair that the school for black students had one room and no glass in the windows. The "white" school in Pine Level had glass windows. It was big and new and built out of bricks. Black students had to bring their own wood to heat their classroom. Their school year was only five or six months long (instead of nine), so that they could work in the cotton fields. The white children who lived near her rode school buses and sometimes threw garbage out the window at black kids, who had to walk. (When she was old enough to understand that black people's taxes helped pay for that white school and its buses, she knew it was *really* unfair.) Some white children in Alabama had terribly poor schools too, but there were almost no good schools for black children.

Why did students at Rosa's school have to bring all their books home every night?

Because the Ku Klux Klan might burn the school down.

The Ku Klux Klan (KKK) is a white American terrorist organization that still exists. Its name is mysterious, but some people think "Ku Klux" comes from the Greek word meaning "circle" or "ring," because the KKK made a circle that shut out black people. Klan is "clan" spelled with a *k*.

The KKK was started after the Civil War ended. In 1865 Southern cities, farms, railroads, and private houses were in ruins. Abraham Lincoln had been assassinated, and under President Andrew Johnson the federal government pardoned most Southern whites. Although the U.S. Congress passed three constitutional amendments protecting the rights of blacks, the Southern state governments passed "black codes." These allowed whites to whip black employees and to jail unemployed black people. Thousands of blacks were murdered. The federal government passed the Reconstruction Acts in 1867 and sent in federal troops to protect blacks and reorganize state governments.

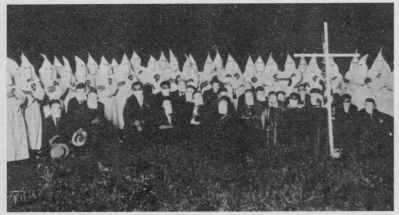

A KKK rally

It was at this time that furious segregationists formed the KKK. Many Southerners wanted to stop the newly freed slaves from enjoying the rights they had gained. Members of the Klan dressed in white ghostlike costumes that hid their faces. They said they were the ghosts of Confederate soldiers. They burned crosses on people's lawns, burned down houses and barns, and beat or killed black citizens—and, sometimes, white citizens who supported blacks' rights.

LANDMARK CONSTITUTIONAL AMENDMENTS

In the 1857 case of *Dred Scott v. Sanford*, the Supreme Court had said that blacks had "no rights which the white man is bound to respect." But after the Civil War ended, three new amendments were added to the Constitution of the United States:

- Thirteenth Amendment (1865): Abolished slavery

- Fourteenth Amendment (1870): No laws could be made that unfairly denied citizens' rights. Everyone had a right to a fair trial and to "equal protection under the law."

- Fifteenth Amendment (1870): A citizen could not be prevented from voting because of his race or because he had been a slave. (A citizen *could* be prevented from voting for not being a "he": Women couldn't vote until 1920. And Indians didn't get the right to vote until 1924. Even then, many states prevented them from registering.)

Because of these amendments, freed men of color could now—in theory—be elected to government office and serve on juries. Fair trials, voting, serving on juries, and protection by the law are "civil rights"—the rights and responsibilities of citizens. But it would be many years before these rights would become a reality for blacks.

When was summer a time of fear?

In Georgia, in 1918, a black veteran, his wife, and two of their friends were gunned down for no reason except that someone didn't like the way a black man looked in a United States Army uniform. One of the bodies had 180 bullet holes in it.

In 1919, when Rosa was six, World War I ended and the black soldiers came home in large numbers. Some historians call that summer the "Red Summer of 1919"—red for the fires of riots in the North and the blood of murders in the South.

Rosa's grandfather stayed up all night with his shotgun on his lap to protect his family. Rosa stayed up with him—if there was going to be any shooting, she wanted to see it, she said. She was brave. But when she was a grown-up woman, she often had trouble sleeping. Rosa wonders if it started with those nights when she was too scared to sleep.

Why was the KKK becoming stronger when Rosa was a girl?

White segregationists feared that black soldiers fighting in World War I were going to get "uppity" when they came home. The Klan had also added Catholics, Jews, and immigrants to its hate list, and membership spread around the country. By 1921 more than one million people belonged to the Klan. By 1924 four million people had joined.

Rosa learned early what it meant to be black in the South. "By the time I was six, I was old enough to realize that we were not actually free," she said. "The Ku Klux Klan was riding through the black community, burning churches, beating up people, killing people."

Why didn't Rosa learn to hate white people, like her grandfather did?

As a child she understood why her grandfather was so angry, and she was also frightened of the KKK. But she didn't feel that all white people were bad just because some were. One old white woman in Pine Level used to take Rosa fishing. The woman visited with Rosa's grandparents and was always respectful toward them. As a very young child, Rosa played with white children. There was also a family story about the day a white soldier from the North patted her on the head and said she was cute—just as though she were a white child. These small acts of respect and kindness showed Rosa that people, no matter what color they were, could behave well or badly.

CHAPTER 2

Breaking the Rules

Was Rosa always a "good girl"?

When Rosa was ten, a white boy raised his fist at her. She picked up a brick and said that if he punched her, she'd hit him with it. He didn't punch her. Rosa was proud of having stood up for herself as her grandfather had taught her, but her grandmother was angry—and frightened. She told Rosa if she "talked back" to white folks, she'd be lynched before she was twenty.

Rosa and other blacks really were putting themselves in danger when they fought back. One day a bunch of white boys threw rocks at Rosa's brother and his friend, who threw some rocks back. Sylvester hit one of the boys but didn't hurt him. A little later the white boys returned with a man who had a gun. The man asked one white boy if these were the black boys who'd thrown the rocks. If the white boy said yes, the man was ready to shoot Sylvester and his friend. Their families would have buried their bodies without being able to go to the police. That's what happened when whites killed blacks, and it happened often. Sylvester never knew why, but the white boy said no. So the man and the boys went away.

Who Was "Judge Lynch"?

Between 1880 and 1968, about five thousand blacks were murdered—shot, tortured, burned alive, chopped apart with knives, and hung from trees—by white mobs. The people killed had not been given trials. Some were taken from their homes, not knowing what crimes they were accused of, and killed along with their families. Others were taken from jails by mobs. Most were "guilty" only of having annoyed a white person—by "talking back" or not being respectful enough, for instance. These mob killings were called lynchings. If these murders were reported to the police, the courts always said the same thing: The victims died "at the hands of persons unknown." Many times lynchings were announced ahead of time so that children could leave school to watch them. People sold photographs of lynchings, and the killers didn't even hide their faces. The message to black Americans was clear: The courts and the government would do nothing to protect them.

When Rosa's grandmother warned Rosa that she could be lynched for talking back to white folks, she meant it. "Judge Lynch" was not a real judge in a courtroom, but the will of a mob, which could sentence a black person to death at any time, for any reason.

Why did Rosa move to the city of Montgomery?

When Rosa's Pine Level school closed, she went to the Spring Hill school, where her mother taught. She walked the long eight miles there and eight miles home every day she was healthy enough to go. But after Rosa turned eleven, there was no school for her to attend. Even if she walked all day, she couldn't reach a school that would teach black seventh graders. So in 1924 Rosa's mother sent her to live with her aunt and cousins in Montgomery, where she could study at the Montgomery Industrial School for Black Girls—a private school often called "Miss White's." Rosa's mother took in sewing and cleaned people's houses—in addition to teaching—to pay for Rosa to go there.

The three hundred girls who went to Miss White's got the best education available to them in that part of Alabama at that time. Miss Alice L. White and her teachers were white women from New England. They believed that if the Southern states were going to deny a good education to black Americans, then it was up to the rest of the country to help out. The school was paid for not just by tuition money but by donations from people in the North. Southern churches also contributed.

Most Southern whites wanted the Northerners to mind their own business. Local whites wouldn't even speak to Miss White and the teachers. They had already burned the school down twice, but Miss White had it rebuilt. The classes Rosa attended were in a sturdy, modern brick building.

What Made the "Roaring Twenties" Roar?

When Rosa moved from Pine Level to Montgomery in the 1920s, she saw a new world—new to her and to everyone else. Montgomery had trains, trolleys, and enough cars for traffic jams. Even if Rosa's aunt's house didn't have "modern conveniences," houses and businesses in the center of the city had electric lights, radios, telephones, and indoor flush toilets.

In 1920 women got the vote. Skirts got short—just below the knee! Women's hair got short—men were shocked! (One barber in California put up a sign: "Barber Shop for Men Only.") Young women started smoking and wearing makeup—mothers fainted! Selling alcohol had been made illegal in 1919, which made drinking more fashionable than ever. Movies (called "talkies") got sound. Music got loud, and dances got fast. World War I was over—and the country wanted to party.

The 1920s, often called "the Jazz Age," were also the time of the Harlem Renaissance. Harlem, in New York City, was a place of hope for blacks. Artists including writer Zora Neale Hurston, poet Langston Hughes, painter William H. Johnson, composer Duke Ellington, and actor Paul Robeson were among the talents who lived, worked, and partied there, creating an explosion of the arts.

Did Rosa always follow all the rules?

At Miss White's school, Rosa learned English, history, geography, math, and science. She was also taught a lot of "domestic science," such as how to cook from scratch, make clothes, and take care of sick people. It was a practical education. Miss White believed that well-educated girls would make better lives for themselves, their families, and their whole communities. It was also an education that would prepare the girls to be teachers, like Rosa's mother. Booker T. Washington liked Miss White's school a lot. So did Rosa.

The 1920s may have been a time of short skirts and wild dances, but not at Miss White's school. The school kept its rules from when it was founded in the late 1800s. Red lipstick, wild dances, and sexy songs were not going to help young women earn respect. Miss White's students wore neat polka-dotted uniforms. They couldn't dance, wear makeup, see movies, straighten their hair, drink alcohol, or wear big earrings. They read the Bible and prayed every day. All this was fine with Rosa. Other girls would go dancing or see a movie, but she wouldn't. Her classmates respected her, but Rosa didn't make close friends easily. She was shy.

Miss White's rules taught self-respect, so Rosa followed them. But the rules of the South, which said that white people were better than black ones, insulted her self-respect. Rosa broke them every time she could. During her first year at Miss White's school, a white boy on roller skates tried to push her off the sidewalk. She pushed him back. The boy's mother said she'd have Rosa put in jail. Rosa told the woman that she hadn't done anything to deserve being pushed, and she didn't want to be pushed. "Nobody ever bossed Rosa around and got away with it," said a childhood friend. Rosa trusted herself to know the difference between good rules and bad rules.

❝ What I learned best at Miss White's school was that I was a person with dignity and self-respect, and I should not set my sights lower than anybody else just because I was black. We were taught to be ambitious and to believe that we could do what we wanted in life. This was not something I learned just at Miss White's school. I learned it from my grandparents and my mother too. **"**

—**Rosa Parks**, as quoted in her autobiography, *Rosa Parks: My Story*, 1992

What *didn't* Rosa learn in school?

"They didn't talk to us much about color," one of Rosa's classmates said. Although the girls were taught not to feel limited by being black, they weren't taught to be proud of their color either. The school's goal was to prove that color didn't matter. Rosa believed in the teachings of Booker T. Washington and Miss White: She believed that people—especially black people—who didn't get enough respect needed to be ultrarespectable. Miss White couldn't have taught her students to defy the laws of the South—they would have been killed—but the students were taught the meaning of racial equality. Many of Miss White's students grew up to work for Civil Rights.

Rosa said later that she wished her high school had taught her more about Sojourner Truth and Harriet Tubman. These Civil War–era heroines risked their lives working on the "Underground Railroad"—the illegal network of workers and hiding places that had smuggled enslaved blacks to free states or Canada. They fought for an end to slavery and also for the rights of women. Rosa said, "They both exemplified a Godly spirit, self-determination, and a willingness to make any sacrifice necessary to free African Americans from slavery."

A segregated water fountain in North Carolina

Who was "Jim Crow"?

Many Southern whites thought of blacks as property—*their* property—which had been "stolen" from them when the slaves were freed during the Civil War. Most Southerners had not owned slaves, yet every time they saw a free black person, it felt like an insult. No Yankee was going to tell them how to treat "their coloreds." Many people truly believed that the black race was inferior to the white race, and a few wrote "scientific studies" to prove it.

Others didn't hate black people, but they needed cheap labor. They were worried about finding cotton pickers to work on their plantations. Black doctors and lawyers weren't going to pick for them.

After federal troops were withdrawn from the South in 1877, the Southern states made new laws, designed to keep the freed black people from feeling free or having civil rights. Nicknamed the "Jim Crow" laws, they *segregated* blacks and whites. Laws forced black people to sit in separate train cars from white people. There were also separate schools, libraries, public bathrooms, drinking fountains, churches, phone booths, and cemeteries. Signs said, "For Whites Only" or "For Coloreds." Black people had to sit in the back of buses and trolleys.

Jim Crow laws varied from state to state. In South Carolina it was illegal for black and white cotton-mill workers to look out the same window. In Birmingham, Alabama, it was illegal for a white person and a black person to play checkers together. There were also laws that kept blacks from being able to vote, even though the Fifteenth Amendment said they could.

Some white people thought segregation was wrong, but there weren't enough of them to change the laws.

THE REAL JIM CROW

In 1828 a white entertainer named Thomas Dartmouth "Daddy" Rice wrote a "blackface" song and dance act. In a blackface act, a white man blackened his face with burned cork or makeup and pretended to be a black man—usually a sort of stupid, happy black man. Rice sang:

"Weel a-bout and turn a-bout

And do just so

Every time I weel about

I jump Jim Crow."

What happened when Jim Crow met Homer Plessy?

A group of educated black citizens of New Orleans, Louisiana, decided to test the segregation laws. So in 1892 a middle-class man named Homer Plessy allowed himself to be arrested for sitting in the "white" part of the train. (Plessy was actually only one-eighth black, but he was still not allowed to sit with the whites.) His lawyers argued that if blacks and whites had equal rights, then the train company couldn't arrest Plessy for sitting in a seat he had paid for. The case, called *Plessy v. Ferguson*, finally went to the Supreme Court, the highest court in the United States.

The Supreme Court's job is to interpret the Constitution and defend the constitutional rights of citizens. The Supreme Court can say when a law, or something a lower court has done, is unconstitutional. But the court is made up of nine human beings and, in 1896, they weren't interested in Civil Rights. Eight of the Supreme Court judges

34

decided it was okay if train cars for blacks and whites were separate as long as they were "separate but equal."

Plessy's lawyers had argued that separate seating was intended to be unequal, but only Justice John Martin Harlan agreed that segregation was wrong. He said the Fourteenth and Fifteenth Amendments were meant to make black people truly equal. Justice Harlan also argued that if the Supreme Court said "separate but equal" was okay on trains, the states would make more and more laws about where blacks could go and take away more and more of their rights.

AMERICAN VOICES

❝ If the two races are to meet, it must be as a result of the voluntary consent of individuals. ❞

—The U.S. Supreme Court in their ruling on *Plessy v. Ferguson*, 1896

❝ We boast of the freedom enjoyed by our people above all other peoples. But it is difficult to reconcile that boast with a state of law which, practically, puts the brand of servitude and degradation upon a large class of our fellow citizens, our equals under the law. ❞

—Justice **John Martin Harlan**, giving his dissenting opinion in *Plessy v. Ferguson*, 1896

Why didn't Rosa Parks learn about Jim Crow laws until she lived in Montgomery?

Pine Level was too small to have water fountains or buses; it only had three stores, and everyone used them. It couldn't have separate waiting rooms at the train station because it was too small to have a train station. It *did* have separate schools and churches.

Montgomery was the state capital and one of the biggest cities in the state. It had been the first capital of the Confederacy and was still called "the cradle of the Confederacy." And it was segregated. In Montgomery Rosa wondered (like all black kids, she says) if "white" water and "black" water tasted different. In Montgomery Rosa would meet up with her cousin Annie Mae after school, and once they stopped for a glass of soda pop. The white woman behind the counter told Annie Mae she could buy an ice-cream cone instead. Annie Mae and Rosa didn't understand. So the woman whispered, "We don't sell sodas to colored people." Annie Mae could stand and eat an ice-cream cone outside, but she couldn't sit at the counter and drink a glass of soda pop.

Was segregation only in the South?

For many Southern blacks, the North seemed like a land of freedom. Northern states had segregation laws before the Civil War, but by the time Rosa was born they didn't have separate drinking fountains or "white only" public parks. Blacks and whites sat together on buses and in movie theaters. It was easier for blacks to vote in the North. So Northern blacks weren't constantly reminded that they were looked down upon.

Yet in Pine Level, Rosa played with the white children who lived next door. In the North whites and blacks more often lived in separate neighborhoods. When a Northern white family signed a contract to buy a house, part of the contract often said they couldn't ever sell the house to blacks or Jews. These contracts kept neighborhoods segregated. Since the schools were neighborhood schools, the schools were segregated too—although not by law and not always. As in the South, many jobs in the North were also "white only." As blacks who left the South discovered, the North had fewer daily humiliations, but it was not a place where blacks and whites lived together in real equality.

THE GREAT SUNTAN CRAZE

In the late 1920s, some "white only" hotels had a problem. Suntans were a new fashion then. So how could the hotels keep out light-skinned, blond-haired "black" people without insulting any of the brown-skinned, dark-haired "white" people? Some hotels in Washington, D.C., hired people to stand in the lobbies and try to figure out who was black and who was white.

What did Rosa Parks think about racism?

As a child she knew that segregated schools were unfair. As an adult she refused to use segregated water fountains. She would go thirsty instead. She would take the stairs instead of using segregated elevators. She believed that racism is un-Christian (because we are all children of God) and un-American (because the Constitution says that everyone should be treated equally by the law).

Rosa knew that it was wrong for people to be treated differently because they happened to be born black. She had also seen how silly racism could be. Strangers thought her light-skinned brother was from Asia. Her grandfather looked white but was so proud of his African roots that he tried to join a political movement started by a man named Marcus Garvey. A black man from the island of Jamaica, Garvey said that real freedom for blacks could be found only if they returned to Africa. But when Rosa's grandfather went to a meeting, the leaders threw him out, saying the ex-slave looked "too white."

AMERICAN VOICES

66 As we learn about one another, we will know that the things we have in common are greater than our differences. . . . Justice and truth do not see color. **99**

—**Rosa Parks**

BLUE EYES/BROWN EYES

On April 5, 1968, the day after Martin Luther King Jr. was assassinated, a third-grade teacher in an all-white town in Iowa began to teach her students about racism. On questioning, the students said that Dr. King was a hero, but they believed that black people were dirty and dishonest. They'd never met a black person, but their parents said black people were like that. The teacher, Jane Elliott, told her students about a "scientific study" (that she had just invented). It showed that brown-eyed children were better than blue-eyed children. Brown-eyed children were smarter, she said, and "blueys" were dumb and lazy and wouldn't be allowed to drink from the water fountain. Within an hour formerly bright, happy, blue-eyed students were having trouble doing their work and feeling lousy. Some of the brown-eyed children did better work than they'd ever done before. They were mean to the "blueys," even to kids who were their friends. The next day the teacher said she'd made a mistake. It was blue-eyed children who were smarter. Soon the blue-eyed children were doing better schoolwork and the "brown eyes" were getting pushed around. Then the teacher talked to the students about why something meaningless like eye color could affect their work and their relationships. The children had learned—fast—what it meant to be racist and how it felt to be discriminated against.

Why did Rosa leave high school?

When Rosa's mother couldn't pay her tuition at Miss White's school any longer, Rosa cleaned classrooms to pay for her schooling. But Miss White had to close her school in 1928, the year Rosa finished eighth grade. Miss White couldn't get new teachers to come to a school in a city that would call them "Yankee nigger lovers."

For ninth grade Rosa went to Montgomery's black public junior high school, Booker T. Washington Junior High. For grades ten and part of eleven, she went to the only black high school around—the laboratory school at the Alabama State Teachers' College for Negroes. Black women who were studying to be teachers taught classes there. A classmate of Rosa's remembers her as a "quiet," "self-composed," "dignified" girl "who did not seek to outshine anyone in the classroom but was always prepared."

Although her mother had wanted her to be a teacher and she had thought of being a nurse, Rosa had to leave school when she was sixteen. Her grandfather had died when she was ten, and now her grandmother had become sick. Rosa went back to Pine Level to take care of her. Grandma Rose died a month later, but then Rosa's mother got sick. Rosa wasn't happy about leaving school, but she felt it was her responsibility. "It was just something that had to be done," she said later.

WHAT'S IN A NAME?

Slaves didn't have their own names. They were given the last name of their owner. In the twentieth century, black women working for white women were sometimes called Mary or other names their employers found easy to remember, rather than by their given names. Grown men were often called "Boy."

When Rosa was growing up, a white five-year-old would call a black minister by his first name. The same child would not have been allowed to call a white adult by his or her first name. It was disrespectful.

Another way white people would insult blacks was to call them "niggers." "Nigger" is now considered so bad that the computer program used to write this book refused to recognize it as a word, and many books and newspapers will write it as "the *N* word." "Negro" was the most polite word for blacks when Rosa was growing up.

CHAPTER 3

From Booker T. to the NAACP

People wait in line for voter registration.

How did Rosa meet her husband?

When Rosa was eighteen, a friend introduced her to Raymond Parks, a twenty-eight-year-old barber in Montgomery. Raymond, who was always called Parks, liked Rosa right away, but she wasn't interested in going out with him. She wasn't looking for romance. Also, she didn't find light-skinned men like Parks attractive. So Rosa was polite to him (because she has always been polite to anyone who is polite to her) and that—she thought—was that.

How did Parks get Rosa to change her mind?

Parks took her for rides in his red sports car, and she got to know him. It was unusual for a black man in the 1930s to own a car, let alone a red sports car—but Raymond Parks was an unusual man.

His father, a white carpenter, had abandoned his family when Raymond was young—just as Rosa's father had. Raymond grew up in an all-white neighborhood, but he couldn't go to the white school because he was half black. His mother, who later remarried, taught him at home. When Raymond was in his teens, his mother and grandmother died and his stepfather threw him out of the house. So he went to work, and then learned to be a barber.

A black barbershop wasn't just a place to get a haircut and a shave. It was a public place where blacks could hang out and talk honestly without any white people overhearing their conversations. It was a place where people could read political magazines and black newspapers. Parks had educated himself;

his reading included many black newspapers and the work of black poets such as Langston Hughes and James Weldon Johnson. Many people who met Parks thought he had gone to college. Like Rosa's grandfather, he was interested in politics and Civil Rights. And like Rosa's grandfather, Parks wasn't afraid of white people. Rosa was impressed.

During their car rides, Rosa realized that Parks was the first person she'd met who was actively working to change the way blacks lived. Rosa's family and the teachers at Miss White's school wanted black people to improve themselves, but Parks wanted to improve the laws of the country. He belonged to the National Association for the Advancement of Colored People—called the "N-double A-C-P."

WHEN WAS THE NAACP FOUNDED?

The NAACP was founded on February 12, 1909—one hundred years from the day of Abraham Lincoln's birth—by both black and white people. Its leader for many years was W. E. B. DuBois. He had been educated at Fisk University, which was a college for blacks, and then at Harvard University and also in Europe. He was one of the black leaders who spoke out strongly against Booker T. Washington's teachings. Washington wanted black people to earn their own self-respect and to gain the respect of whites gradually, through the way they lived and worked. In contrast, DuBois and the NAACP thought the laws that discriminated against black people had to change immediately. They fought for the rights of blacks to vote and for an end to segregation. In the 1930s they tried (and failed) to make Congress pass laws against lynching. In the 1940s they fought for equal education for blacks and whites. The NAACP often worked through the courts to try to change laws and to get fair trials for black people.

66 We claim for ourselves every single right that belongs to a free American, political, civil and social; and until we get these rights we will never cease to protest and assail the ears of America. 99

—**W. E. B. DuBois**, from his "Address to the Country" speech in which he disagrees with Booker T. Washington, 1905

When did Rosa McCauley become Rosa Parks?

Parks proposed the second time they went out, but Rosa didn't agree to marry him until they had known each other for two years. They got married in December 1932 in Rosa's house in Pine Level. It wasn't a fancy wedding—just a small gathering of family and close friends. Then Mr. and Mrs. Parks went to live in Montgomery.

Parks knew how much his new wife had wanted to finish high school, and he encouraged her to return to the laboratory school. Rosa Parks graduated when she was twenty. Yet although very few black people in Montgomery had a high school diploma, her education didn't help her get a better job. Many jobs were still not open to black people or to women, and the early 1930s were a bad time for the American economy. Rosa Parks worked as a nurse's assistant at a hospital and took in sewing to do at home.

BROTHER, CAN YOU SPARE A DIME?

In the 1930s the United States experienced the Great Depression, the worst economic collapse that the country had ever seen. In 1925 about 3 percent of the workforce (people who would usually be working) were without jobs. In 1933 about 25 percent of the workforce was unemployed. That means one working person out of every four couldn't find a job. Thousands of educated adults shined shoes or sold apples. Families lost their homes and farms because they couldn't pay their bills. Communities of people lived in shacks made of tin cans and wooden boxes around the edges of towns and cities.

People went hungry, but farmers destroyed their crops because they would have had to sell food for less money than it took to raise it. One county courthouse burned corn for heat because it was cheaper than coal. And on top of everything else, there was a drought. In parts of the Midwest, crops and then soil blew right off the land in dust storms. The people blew away too—to look for work in cities (although there wasn't any work there either) or to California to pick fruit and vegetables on farms.

"Brother, Can You Spare a Dime?" was a popular song in the 1930s—the trouble was, almost no one had any dimes to spare.

Who were the Scottsboro Boys?

When Parks began dating Rosa, he was working on the case of the "Scottsboro Boys." The Scottsboro case was about everything that was the matter with the way the legal system was working—or not working—for Southern blacks.

In the 1930s, when the Great Depression had caused many people to lose their jobs and homes, people traveled the country looking for work. The Scottsboro boys were nine young blacks, ages thirteen to nineteen, who had hitched a ride on a freight train from Tennessee to Alabama one day in 1931. Some white hobos threw gravel at them and told them to get off the train; they fought back and threw the whites off the train instead. The white hobos then beat the train to the next station and complained to the police. When the train stopped, the police arrested the nine boys. The police took them to jail in Scottsboro, Alabama, and charged them with assault. The next day two white prostitutes who had also been taken off the train said that the boys had beaten and raped them and threatened them with guns and knives.

A group of black preachers hired a lawyer, but he spent only a half hour with his nine clients. After a three-day trial, in which two doctors said the women hadn't been beaten or hurt in any way and no one was able to produce a single gun or knife used in the supposed attacks, the judge made it clear that he thought the nine were guilty. A white jury sentenced all the boys but one to die in the electric chair. (The youngest boy was sent to jail instead.)

Raymond Parks said that he would have trouble sleeping at night until the Scottsboro boys were free.

Could this kind of unfair trial really happen in the United States?

Trials like this happened often in the South, but this case made the newspapers around the country and the NAACP took the case to the Supreme Court. The Supreme Court said it was an unfair trial because the young men's lawyer didn't do his job, so the state of Alabama had another trial that didn't end until 1937. This time three young men were freed, but five were sent to jail. The last of the young men didn't get out of jail until 1950—nineteen years after he hadn't done anything wrong.

Why didn't Rosa Parks join the meetings of the National Committee to Defend the Scottsboro Boys?

Raymond Parks said they were too dangerous. When the committee met, someone always had to be the lookout. They met in different places and didn't use one another's real names. If the police came, they'd have to run. Rosa Parks wrote about one meeting that was held at her house. She sat on the back porch, with her face down on her knees. She had seen the table covered with guns: all those guns so that a group of black men could hold a meeting. She hated it. It was too much like sitting up at night with her grandfather and his gun when she was six, waiting to see if this was the night that the KKK was going to come after them.

Where did Rosa Parks get a first glimpse of what integration could be like?

World War II began in Europe in 1939, but the United States did not join the fight until the Japanese bombed Pearl Harbor, a U.S. military base in Hawaii, in 1941. The war created many jobs, and Rosa Parks got one as a secretary on Maxwell Field, an army air force base just outside Montgomery. Soon after Raymond Parks got a job there as a barber. It wasn't possible for a black person to work at the base before the war. But President Franklin D. Roosevelt had desegregated military bases in 1941, although the army itself was still segregated. (President Truman desegregated the military in 1948.)

At the base Rosa Parks could eat in an integrated lunchroom and sit anywhere she pleased on an integrated trolley. But once she left the base and got on a bus to go home, she had to ride in the back. Sometimes on the base she rode with a white woman and the woman's son. The boy would see the women sitting together on the trolley, talking, and then see Rosa Parks walk to the back of the city bus. Rosa wrote that from the way he looked at her, the boy must have thought this was very strange. The segregated bus became "a humiliation" to her.

Why did Rosa Parks join the NAACP in 1943?

Her husband had belonged to the NAACP for nine years, so Rosa Parks knew a lot about the organization. Raymond Parks was pleased that his wife was joining, but he was also nervous, because being an NAACP member could get you lynched. He also felt that NAACP members, many of them business owners and professionals (like doctors and ministers), didn't have enough respect for "workingmen" like himself.

But the NAACP *had* persuaded President Roosevelt to integrate military bases, like the one where Raymond and Rosa Parks worked. Rosa was also impressed by the work being done by Walter White, a Northern NAACP leader. Because he was blond and blue eyed, White could travel to places where there had been lynchings and talk to the people who had committed the crimes. Pretending to be white, he would let people brag to him about the murders they had committed. One man complained that it had taken fifty bullets to kill one black woman. White was risking his life so that he could write and lecture about lynchings and try to make Congress pass laws against them.

There was another, more personal reason why Rosa Parks went to an NAACP meeting one day in 1943. She had seen a picture in the newspaper of an old friend from Miss White's school—Johnnie Mae Carr—at a meeting and wanted to see her again. The women did become reacquainted, although on the day of Rosa's first NAACP meeting, Johnnie Mae Carr wasn't in attendance. Rosa was the only woman there. The men elected her secretary and, since she was too polite and shy to say no, she just started taking notes.

Parks left the NAACP about the time that his wife joined, but he continued to work on Civil Rights issues.

What work did Rosa Parks do for the Montgomery NAACP?

For the next twelve years, Rosa Parks was the Montgomery NAACP's volunteer secretary, organizer, researcher, and historian. She worked with the man who soon became the local NAACP president, E. D. Nixon. She answered mail, took notes of everything that happened in meetings, and wrote letters for Nixon. Like Walter White, she read newspapers and gathered information about the beatings, tortures, rapes, and murders of black people. When a black minister saw a white man shoot a black man, Rosa Parks went and talked to the minister about testifying in court, but he was too afraid to say what he had seen. She learned of horrible things that she couldn't do anything about—but at least the NAACP could report these events in their magazine, *The Crisis.*

Another part of Rosa Parks's work for the NAACP involved making it possible for black people to vote. This was something Parks was particularly interested in too.

How Did E. D. Nixon Become an NAACP Organizer?

One of seventeen children, E. D. Nixon left school early to work on the railroad as a sleeping-car porter. Travel soon became his education. In the North he ate in integrated restaurants and walked on sidewalks where a black man did not have to lower his eyes and step out of the way when a white woman walked by. These experiences may have inspired him to fight for equal rights. In 1927 he joined a union of black railroad workers under the leadership of A. Philip Randolph and quickly became one of Montgomery's leading organizers of its new NAACP chapter. Montgomery's educated black professionals found him a little hard to take. Unlike Raymond Parks, E. D. Nixon never sounded like a college graduate—but he got results. Rosa Parks called him "a proud, dignified man who carried himself straight as an arrow."

Why did Rosa and Raymond Parks and the NAACP believe the right to vote was so important?

Southern local and state governments made the segregation laws. Southern judges wouldn't give blacks fair trials. The NAACP was trying to change the laws by taking court cases to the Supreme Court, where the decisions would be fairer. But another way to change bad laws is to vote for people who will make better ones. When you vote, you choose the people who make laws and run the government. Being able to vote for the people in our government is what makes the United States a democracy. But most Southern blacks couldn't vote. Even men like Rosa's brother, Sylvester McCauley, who had been drafted and served in World War II, couldn't vote. So those who supported segregation laws and unfair trials continued to be elected.

Why was it so hard for blacks to vote?

Before people can vote, they have to *register*, or sign up. Southern whites made it nearly impossible for blacks to register. (In fact, when Rosa Parks began to work on voter registration, she found there were only thirty-one black people registered in Montgomery—and some of them were dead.) Voter registration offices for blacks would open for just a few hours at a time and not let anyone know when they'd open. There would be long lines, so someone might wait for two hours and then be told that the office was closed. People were lynched for helping blacks register to vote.

Southern states also had laws that said all people had to own property to vote or pass a test and pay a poll tax. But white people decided who passed the test, and they didn't have to explain why someone failed. In 1943 Rosa Parks was told that she failed the test—even though she was much more educated than most people were at that time. Raymond Parks was never able to register in the state of Alabama. White people who knew him offered to help, but he refused to be registered that way. He wanted the rules to change.

What happened the second time that Rosa Parks tried to register to vote in 1943?

She wasn't able to register, *and* she got thrown off a bus for not obeying the bus driver.

Segregation of water fountains was humiliating, but it was simple: One had a sign saying "Whites," and the other had a sign saying "Coloreds." Buses, however, were humiliating *and* complicated. Every city had different rules about who could sit where. In fact, every bus in the same city could have different rules, because the driver could make up rules—and he carried a gun to enforce them.

In Montgomery the front ten bus seats were for whites. Even if there wasn't a single white person on the bus and all the other seats were full, no black person could sit on those seats. The back ten seats were for blacks—unless the other seats filled up and a white person needed a seat. The middle sixteen

> ### A REAL VOTING TEST: CAN YOU PASS IT?
>
> *How many bubbles are there in a bar of soap?*
>
> Not sure? Too bad. You can't vote.
>
> This was a real question that was used to keep blacks from registering. Other questions weren't ridiculous; they were just difficult. People would have to answer questions about state laws that were so hard a lawyer might not be able to answer them. Even if you had the answers right, like Rosa Parks, the white person scoring a test could just say you failed.

seats were for everyone, except that if a white person needed a seat, the whole row of black passengers would have to get up, because a white person couldn't sit in a row that had black people in it.

That's the simple part.

Most drivers would make black people pay their fare, then get off and get on the bus again through the back door. If the driver was feeling mean, he would wait until someone had paid and gotten off and then drive away. Some drivers were verbally abusive and some hit or punched people. Sometimes they shot them. One driver closed the bus door on a black man and then dragged him along the road.

After Rosa Parks tried to register to vote for the second time, she got on a bus. The driver was named James Blake, although she wouldn't know that for another twelve years. Rosa Parks paid her ten cents, but the back of the bus was so crowded that it would be impossible to get on using the back stairs. There were only a few people standing in front, so she walked toward the back of the bus and stood there. Blake said she could either get off the bus and use the back stairs, or just get off and stay off. When Rosa Parks stood quietly in place, the driver got up and took her coat sleeve to push her off the bus. She didn't struggle, but when they reached the front of the bus, she "accidentally" dropped her purse. Then she sat on a "white only" seat to pick it up. The furious driver said, "Get off my bus." Rosa Parks believed he was going to hit her. "I will get off," she said. "You better not hit me." Then she left. After that, she avoided the bus driven by Blake.

Did the other black people on the bus help Rosa Parks?

No. She heard someone grumble, "She ought to go around the back and get on." People were tired, she says, and they wanted to get home. And, she says, blacks were not used to fighting back. Fighting back was dangerous, and it didn't help. A lot of people had given up. They just wanted to try to stay out of trouble. They felt hopeless, because there seemed to be nothing they could do to make their lives better. Booker T. Washington taught that if black people were hardworking and well mannered, they would earn respect. It wasn't working.

How were Southern black World War II veterans treated when they returned home in 1945?

The same way they'd been treated after World War I: They were beaten up and killed for being too "uppity." No one would give them jobs. Segregationists  spat at them. A black veteran in a uniform with medals for bravery was in more danger than a field hand in a pair of dirty overalls. During the war, German prisoners of war worked in fields in the South. Black soldiers guarded some of those prisoners—but if they went into a café for a drink, the enemy prisoners could use the front doors and the American guards had to go around the back.

The U.S. Army was still segregated, but in Europe black soldiers could go into any restaurant. There were no "Whites Only" signs. They fought for democracy and against Hitler's "white supremacy"—and then came home to a country that still taught white supremacy. (Hitler and American segregationists agreed that Jews and Catholics weren't "real" whites.) Sylvester McCauley had worked for a medical unit, saving the lives of other soldiers, black and white. Yet when he came home, he wasn't allowed to vote and he couldn't get a job. When he saw how black veterans were treated, he moved his family to Detroit, Michigan. Many other black veterans did the same thing. More than half the jobs in Detroit were still "white only" and there had been race riots two years earlier, but it was still a better place for a black war veteran to make a life for himself than in the South. Rosa Parks visited her brother there and rode her first integrated city buses—but her life and work were in Montgomery.

AMERICAN VOICES

66 The army jim-crows us. The Navy lets us serve only as messmen [kitchen workers]. The Red Cross refuses our blood. Employers and unions shut us out. Lynchings continue. We are disenfranchised, jim-crowed, spat upon. What more could Hitler do than that? 99

—The words of a black soldier after World War II, as repeated by NAACP leader Walter White

When was Rosa Parks able to register to vote?

In 1945 she wrote out a copy of her whole exam—
questions and answers—ready to go to court and
prove that she had been illegally denied her right to
register to vote. But this time she received her voter
registration in the mail. The only problem was that
she now had to pay the poll tax for every year since
she'd reached voting age; her total fee was $16.50.
Rosa Parks was making about $25 a week, so $16.50
was a lot of money.

What was Rosa Parks doing for the NAACP during the late 1940s and early 1950s?

Rosa Parks loved children, but she and her husband
were unable to have children of their own. However,
she liked working as the adviser to the NAACP Youth
Council and taught high school students what she
had learned: to believe in their own dignity and
rights. She also taught them to protest segregation.
Over and over again, the students would try to

borrow books from the main library instead of from the small "colored" library. Each time they were denied. Southern segregationists said that "their" Negroes were happy, and it was only outsiders who stirred things up. But every time the Youth Council members politely explained why they should be able to borrow a book from the main library, they were showing that they were *not* happy with segregation.

In 1949 Rosa Parks quit being secretary of the NAACP for about two years because her mother, who now lived with them, was sick. But she continued to work for E. D. Nixon at his union office and at the offices of the black Democratic association.

Rosa Parks had noticed how few other women were members of the NAACP—just her mother and Johnnie Mae Carr. "Women don't need to be nowhere but in the kitchen," Nixon used to tell her. Rosa Parks would say, "Well, what about me?" He would admit that he needed her to work for him, but the Civil Rights movement wasn't concerned with women's rights. Still, by the late 1940s there were more women in the Civil Rights movement, all over the country. In 1946 Mary Fair Burks founded an organization called the Women's Political Council (WPC) in Montgomery, to work for black voter registration. In 1948, in a speech at the state NAACP convention, Rosa Parks spoke out about the mistreatment of black women in the South. Yet Rosa Parks was mostly a behind-the-scenes person. She worked on whatever needed doing, but she was still shy.

CHAPTER 4

We Shall Overcome

How did a little girl change Rosa Parks's life in 1954?

In 1896 the Supreme Court had said in *Plessy v. Ferguson* that "separate but equal" was the law of the land. But the court can change its mind. Fifty-eight years later, a Supreme Court made up of different judges said "separate but equal" is not constitutional—at least, not in schools. This was the verdict of *Brown v. Board of Education*, one of the most important law cases in American history.

The 1954 case began with a seven-year-old girl named Linda Brown, who lived in Topeka, Kansas. Every day Linda had to walk across railroad tracks and take a long bus ride to school. There was a school right near her house, but she couldn't go there. Linda was black, and the school in her neighborhood was for whites only. Linda's father thought this was wrong, and he sued the Topeka Board of Education.

Linda's case went to the Supreme Court along with some other lawsuits about "separate but equal" education. One case was brought by a whole high school that had gone on a strike organized by a sixteen-year-old student, Barbara Johns.

The court took a long time to decide if separate schools were constitutional. One reason they took so long is that they wanted every judge to agree, because that would make the decision more powerful. To the delight of Rosa Parks and the NAACP—and the horror of the segregationists—the court declared that separate schools could *never* be equal, not even if they had exactly the same number of good teachers and new books. Being separate was enough to make them unequal, said the court. Segregating black children because of their race made them feel unequal and hurt their ability to learn. It was, as Justice John Martin Harlan had said in 1896, unconstitutional. His grandson, also named John Martin Harlan, was one of the justices who helped reach a unanimous decision in the 1954 case.

Why was the Supreme Court decision about school segregation so important?

This was the first time since the 1880s that the federal government had sided with Civil Rights advocates. "It was a very hopeful time," said Rosa

Parks. If this Supreme Court was willing to desegregate the schools, would they be willing to desegregate other things—like buses? Rosa Parks, E. D. Nixon, and the national NAACP all thought so.

Jo Ann Robinson, a black professor at the Alabama State College in Montgomery, also thought the time was right. As president of the Women's Political Council, she wrote a letter to Montgomery's mayor, threatening a boycott if the bus company didn't loosen up its policies. Mayor W. A. Gayle refused to help, but it wasn't clear that a bus boycott would work anyway. When Rosa Parks and other women talked to people about a boycott, many said that they couldn't stay off the buses—they just had too far to travel to work every day.

WHO WAS THURGOOD MARSHALL?

Thurgood Marshall after the Supreme Court decision of *Brown v. Board of Education*

Thurgood Marshall studied under Charles Houston, who trained a generation of black Civil Rights lawyers. In 1946 Marshall became head of the NAACP's new Legal Defense Fund. He had already won almost all the cases he had taken in the years before he became the main lawyer for *Brown v. Board of Education*. In 1967 President Johnson appointed him the first black judge ever on the United States Supreme Court, where he served until his retirement in 1991.

The NAACP had a different idea. They didn't want a boycott. They wanted a court case, like *Brown v. Board of Education*. They wanted the Supreme Court to say that city buses had to be desegregated.

What were the White Citizens' Councils?

Claiming to be less violent than the KKK, the White Citizens' Councils of the South formed right after the Supreme Court ruled on *Brown v. Board of Education*. The councils said they would stop black progress through economic threats. Anyone who supported Civil Rights or black advancement would be unable to borrow money to buy a house or find a job.

AMERICAN VOICES

66 When in the course of human events, it becomes necessary to abolish the Negro race, proper methods should be used. Among them are guns, bows and arrows, slingshots, and knives. 99

—White Citizens' Council newsletter, 1954

How did a fifteen-year-old girl help make history?

In March 1955 Claudette Colvin was sitting on a city bus when the driver told her to give up her seat to a white person. Claudette had been thinking for a long time about laws that humiliated black people. She'd written a paper for school about a law that said that black women couldn't try on hats in stores. When she refused to leave her seat, the driver called the police, who dragged Claudette from the bus. She did not go quietly. She yelled, "He has no right. . . . This is my constitutional right. . . .You have no right to do this!" As the police dragged Claudette off that bus, she kicked and bit them—and they hit her with a nightstick.

Why was Rosa Parks interested in Claudette's case?

Claudette was the great-granddaughter of Gus Vaughn—the black man in Pine Level who stood up to the white overseer. Rosa and Claudette's mother had played together when they were children. Rosa thought that Claudette had her great-grandfather's pride.

Also, Rosa and the NAACP thought Claudette's case might be the one they could take to the Supreme Court.

Why couldn't Claudette's case go to the Supreme Court?

The NAACP wanted just the right person for the case: a woman (because a woman would be less scary to whites than a man) who had a good reputation. When E. D. Nixon and the other black leaders heard that Claudette was going to have a baby, they dropped the case. Claudette later said that she wasn't pregnant, but even the rumor made her too much of a risk. The whites would say Claudette was a "bad girl," and the case would be lost. The NAACP couldn't risk years of court cases and the money it would cost on anyone but the perfect plaintiff.

After Claudette was arrested, Jo Ann Robinson, E. D. Nixon, and Fred Gray (one of Montgomery's two black lawyers) brought a petition to the bus company and the city officials, again asking for at least a more polite segregation on the buses. Rosa Parks thought this was a mistake: "I had decided that I would not go anywhere with a piece of paper in my hand asking white folks for any favors." This request for change was refused.

> **WHAT DOES IT MEAN?**
>
> A **petition** is a list of requests or demands. The right to submit a petition is guaranteed by the First Amendment to the Constitution.

In October 1955 eighteen-year-old Mary Louise Smith refused to give up her seat to a white woman. She too was rejected as Supreme Court case material. E. D. Nixon said that the young woman came from a bad family; later Mary Louise would argue that Nixon simply wouldn't risk the case on anyone who was too poor.

Did Rosa Parks have any white friends?

Virginia Foster was born in Alabama but later moved to Massachusetts to attend Wellesley College. She was horrified to learn that the college had a "rotating tables" policy, which meant that everyone had to sit with random groups of students—including black students—in the school dining room. But given a choice between leaving Wellesley and overcoming her beliefs about who was supposed to eat where, Virginia changed her beliefs—fast.

After college she married a wealthy Southern lawyer named Clifford Durr. Together they lost all their money and most of their white friends fighting for Civil Rights in Washington, D.C. When they moved to Montgomery, Virginia Durr needed someone to do some sewing for her. E. D. Nixon introduced her to Rosa Parks, and the two women soon became close friends and political allies. Writing to another friend, Virginia Durr described Rosa Parks as "thoroughly good and brave. . . . When she feels at ease and gets relaxed, she can show a delightful sense of humor, but it is not often."

Where did Rosa Parks go to learn more about Civil Rights?

In 1932 a white man named Myles Horton began the Highlander Folk School in the Appalachian Mountains of Tennessee. He wanted to help poor people from that region fight for safer working conditions and better pay. During the fifties he was working for Civil Rights.

Myles Horton called his friend Virginia Durr and asked if she knew someone who would want to come to a ten-day workshop at Highlander in the summer of 1955. She immediately said, "Rosa Parks."

Even though the Supreme Court had said that schools must be desegregated, it hadn't said when, and most schools were simply ignoring the ruling. Highlander's workshop was about how to get schools to *implement* desegregation. Rosa Parks wanted to go to the workshop because she cared about what happened to the teenagers she worked with. She didn't want to go for herself because, as she told Virginia Durr, "I felt I had been destroyed too long ago." It is one of the rare times when Rosa Parks admitted how she felt about all the ugly things she had seen and experienced and so often been unable to change. She was full of anger and pain.

> **WHAT DOES IT MEAN?**
> To **implement** means to put into practice.

Rosa Parks didn't know the school would be so pretty—there were two hundred acres of fields and gardens—and she didn't know it would be so integrated. People joked that Highlander was the only place in the South where blacks and whites could "tea together and pee together." It was the first place she'd ever been where blacks and whites lived, worked, swam, and played games together as equals. People called one another "brother" and "sister" as they did in her church—"Sister Rosa" or "Brother Myles." Rosa Parks had lived only in places where black people could be killed for calling white people by their first names or "talking back" to them. She found it hard to believe that it was safe for her to talk about the experience of her brother and other black soldiers after the war, and about the lynchings and unfair trials she had documented for the NAACP.

What was Rosa Parks's favorite Highlander memory?

People took turns doing the chores, so when Rosa Parks smelled coffee brewing and bacon frying, it meant that white folks were helping cook breakfast for her. It was "one of my greatest pleasures," she wrote later.

One Highlander teacher named Septima Clark, whose father had been a slave, especially impressed her. Rosa Parks said she hoped some of Septima Clark's "great courage, dignity, and wisdom" would rub off on her. Clark later said, "Rosa Parks was afraid for white people to know that she was as militant as she was." Septima Clark probably understood better than most people that underneath Rosa Parks's quiet, polite manners was the woman who believed she should not have to "take bad treatment from anyone."

Rosa Parks had been feeling hopeless and full of anger toward white people. At Highlander she learned how to laugh again, and some of her anger washed away. As she said years later, "I gained strength there to persevere in my work for freedom, not just for blacks but all oppressed people."

"WE SHALL OVERCOME"

People at the Highlander Folk School wrote "We Shall Overcome," one of the songs later sung during the Montgomery bus boycott and throughout the Civil Rights movement. Like many Civil Rights songs, "We Shall Overcome" was based on a traditional hymn; it was a church song, with its words changed a little. At Civil Rights demonstrations and rallies, singing together calmed people, united them, and gave them hope. It also really confused the people who were screaming, cursing, and throwing rocks at the black demonstrators, as well as the police who were arresting them.

AMERICAN VOICES

❝We shall overcome, we shall overcome,
We shall overcome, someday.
Oh, deep in my heart I do believe,
That we shall overcome someday.❞
—**Zilphia Horton, Frank Hamilton, Guy Carawan,** and
Pete Seeger, 1960

What happened when Rosa Parks went back to Montgomery?

Rosa Parks returned to the heat of a Montgomery summer and worked in the basement of Montgomery Fair department store, in the tailor shop. She went back to a place where a white person could insult a black person and the black person was supposed to *smile*. And she went back to the segregated buses, which were a greater trial than ever after her days at Highlander.

Rosa Parks also heard a young minister make a speech at a small NAACP meeting. His name was Martin Luther King Jr. When people at the meeting heard him speak, they knew he could be a good leader, but no one could imagine how important he would become. And, he said later, he could never have imagined that a woman named Rosa Parks would change his life.

Then, in August 1955, a boy named Emmett Till was murdered.

How did the murder of a teenager change the Civil Rights movement?

Emmett Till was a joke-loving, fourteen-year-old student who went to an all-black school in his hometown of Chicago, Illinois. He didn't understand about Southern segregation, even though his mother had told him over and over again to be careful before he went to Mississippi to visit some relatives. One August day in 1955, during his visit, Emmett, a cousin, and some friends of his cousin went to a store

Emmett Till

to buy soda and candy. Even today it is not clear what happened next. The most serious charge is that when Emmett left the store, he supposedly whistled at the white woman who owned it. We do know he was tortured and shot through the head by the woman's husband and his brother-in-law. A seventy-five-pound cotton-gin fan was attached to his neck with barbed wire, and his body was dumped in the river.

Emmett had been staying with his great-uncle, a sixty-four-year-old man named Mose Wright. When the murderers had come at night to get Emmett, they told Wright, "If you make any trouble, you'll never live to be sixty-five." Usually that would be enough to keep a witness quiet, as Rosa Parks had learned when she tried to find black people who would testify in court. But Mose Wright risked his life by standing in a white court and pointing his finger at the two white men who had committed the murder. Other black witnesses also testified. But the white judge told the jury to say that the men were innocent, and they did. Soon after the two men sold the story of the murder to a newspaper for four thousand dollars. The laws of the United States say that people cannot be put on trial twice for the same crime, so they were safe.

Emmett's mother insisted that her son's funeral be held with the coffin open so that people could see what had been done to him. Fifty thousand men, women, and children in Chicago walked past his coffin. Many fainted at the sight of his crushed and battered head. Pictures of his corpse were printed in newspapers and magazines around the world. People talked about Emmett Till's murder and the trial in churches, on the radio, and on TV.

It was time for change. It had been time for change for a long time.

SEARCHING FOR TRUTH

In May 2004, nearly fifty years after Emmett Till was murdered, the U.S. Justice Department announced it would reopen the case—the first major case in the Civil Rights movement. The chief reason behind the government's decision was the production of two documentary films about Emmett Till's case that both claimed that many more people were involved in this young boy's gruesome death. (The two men who bragged that they did it are now dead.)

One of those films was made by Keith Beauchamp, who became fascinated with the case of Emmett Till when he read the story in *Jet* magazine as a boy. Convinced that a great injustice had been done, he spent nine years and much of his own money collecting information about the case and working on his film. He never gave up, because he was on a mission to find the truth. In his crusade to get the whole story out, Keith Beauchamp finally helped convince members of Congress and the Justice Department to reopen the case. Someday we may know the real story of Emmett Till's death.

Like the story of Rosa Parks herself, the story of Keith Beauchamp working to right a wrong shows how one person can make a difference. It also proves that history is about making sure that the truth comes out.

CHAPTER 5

Tired of Giving In

Rosa Parks on a Montgomery bus

Does it matter who drives the bus?

On Thursday, December 1, 1955, Rosa had been at work all day sewing in the basement tailor shop of the department store. It was a few weeks before Christmas, so the store was busy. Rosa had spent her morning coffee break planning an NAACP workshop. Then, as she often did, she'd eaten lunch with Fred Gray in his law office and done some secretarial work for him. When she got on the bus that evening, she was thinking of other things. She didn't notice that James Blake was driving the bus. He was the driver who had ordered her off the bus twelve years earlier. She took an aisle seat in the first row of "colored" seats.

Why was Rosa Parks arrested?

When Rosa Parks got on the bus, it wasn't full. But after a few stops, all the seats were taken, and one white man was standing. Rosa Parks, the man sitting next to her by the window, and the two women across the aisle were all supposed to get up, because the law said that a black person couldn't even sit in the same row as a white person.

When they didn't get up, James Blake said, "Move y'all, I want those seats."

No one moved.

"Y'all better make it light on yourselves and let me have those seats."

The three other people in the row moved to the back of the bus. Rosa Parks moved her legs out of the way so that the man sitting next to her could get by.

"Are you going to stand up?" asked the driver.

"No," said Rosa Parks.

"Well, I'm going to have you arrested," the driver said.

Rosa Parks looked straight at James Blake. "You may do that," she said quietly.

What was Rosa Parks thinking when she refused to give up her seat?

Rosa Parks has answered that question many times. She knows some people think she was some old lady who sewed clothes and was just tired that day, but it's not true. Rosa Parks wasn't that old (she was only forty-two), and she'd been more tired other days. She says, "The only tired I was, was tired of giving in."

She says she was thinking of those nights when she sat up with her grandfather and his gun, and how all the years of "giving in" to racism hadn't made things better. She was thinking that the only way to show that segregation was wrong was to say no to it, the way she'd been saying no privately by not using segregated water fountains or elevators. She says she wanted "this particular driver to know that we were being treated unfairly as individuals and as a people.

"There had to be a stopping place, and this seemed to be the place to stop being pushed around and find out what human rights I had, if any."

Some white people said that Rosa Parks was planted on the bus by the NAACP to be a "test case" for the Supreme Court. She says, "I did not get on the bus to get arrested. I got on the bus to go home." But Rosa Parks was not just acting on impulse. "I had felt for a long time, that if I was ever told to get up so a white person could sit, that I would refuse to do so," she said later.

TAKING A STAND BY SITTING

Protests against segregated public transportation are as old as public transportation itself. Here are just a few:

c. 1865 Sojourner Truth has a conductor fired for trying to push her off a streetcar in Washington, D.C.

1884 Ida B. Wells, a black newspaper writer, sues the State of Tennessee when she is arrested for refusing to leave her seat in a "white only" train car. (She won her case, but the state supreme court overturned the ruling.)

1892 Homer Plessy is arrested for sitting in a "white only" car on East Louisiana Railroad.

1900 Montgomery blacks boycott the city's trolleys for five weeks, and the trolley company desegregates them. Segregation returns to the trolleys by the 1920s.

1941 Illinois congressman Arthur Mitchell refuses to move to a second-class car on a train that does not have a first-class car for blacks. The Supreme Court says a "separate but equal" car was not offered to him, so the train company is found guilty.

1943 Jackie Robinson is arrested for refusing to move to the back of the bus in Fort Hood, Texas.

1944 Irene Morgan is arrested for not giving up her seat on an interstate bus to a white person. The Supreme Court says that the state cannot interfere with "interstate transportation," but does not overrule *Plessy v. Ferguson*.

1947 Civil Rights pioneer Bayard Rustin goes on a "freedom ride" across the South to test the Supreme Court's ruling on the Morgan case. He is arrested eighteen times and sentenced to several months' labor on a chain gang.

1953 Blacks in Baton Rouge, Louisiana, hold a ten-day bus boycott and succeed in slightly changing the rules for segregated seating on city buses.

What did other people do when Rosa Parks wouldn't get out of her seat?

The driver called his supervisor, who told him to wait for the police. Many passengers got off the bus, nervous about what was going to happen. Rosa Parks remembers people talking in whispers, but other passengers remember total silence. "It was like a mosque," one of them said later. "You could have heard a pin drop." Some people say they knew that something historic was happening, but no one—not even people who knew her—spoke to Rosa or joined in her protest.

Rosa Parks said later, "I knew I had the strength of my ancestors with me." She believed God was with her. Otherwise, she was alone.

What happened when Rosa Parks was arrested?

When the police came, they were not really thrilled to arrest a well-dressed, middle-aged black lady. When one of them asked Rosa why she hadn't gotten up, she asked him, "Why do you all push us around?" He said, "I don't know, but the law is the law, and you're under arrest." The police picked up her purse and her shopping bag, and she went with them to the police car. They didn't touch her or handcuff her. For a moment Rosa Parks was even amused. She thought of times when she was a child when other kids would tease her for being such a good little girl in her clean little white gloves—and here she was being taken off to jail. Later on in the Civil Rights movement, people would proudly bring their toothbrushes to protest marches, knowing they would be arrested. But when Rosa Parks was taken to jail, it was shameful and dangerous. Respectable ladies didn't get arrested, and black people could be beaten or killed in jail.

How was Rosa Parks treated in jail?

When she asked for a drink from the water fountain, one officer said yes, but the other said, "No! You can't drink no water. It's for whites only." They said she couldn't make a phone call. She was photographed and fingerprinted for her police record. Then she was put in a segregated jail cell. One of the women in the cell gave Rosa Parks some water and talked to her. Hearing about the other woman's problems helped Rosa Parks forget about her own for a little while, and the next day she was able to help that woman get out of jail.

After about two hours, she was allowed to call home. Her mother answered the phone, and Rosa Parks said, "I'm in jail. See if Parks will come down here and get me out." Her mother and husband were afraid she'd been beaten, but she said no, she was fine. She just needed Parks to get her out of there.

Even before Parks was able to get to the jail, other people arrived. One woman who had seen Rosa Parks taken off the bus told E. D. Nixon's wife what had happened, and she told Nixon. He called the police station to find out if Rosa Parks was okay and what she had been charged with, but the police wouldn't talk to him because he was black. So Nixon called Clifford Durr, and Durr found out that she had been arrested for breaking the segregation laws. Bail was one hundred dollars. Durr didn't have it, but Nixon did, so the two men and Virginia Durr went to the jail.

Virginia Durr was the first person Rosa Parks saw. With tears in her eyes, Virginia hugged and kissed Rosa—"as if we were sisters," Rosa said later. Parks also had tears in his eyes when he arrived. He hugged her so hard that her feet left the ground. Virginia Durr later said that she was impressed with how calm Rosa was, but Rosa didn't feel very calm. "I didn't realize how much being in jail had upset me until I got out," she wrote later.

Before leaving the jail, Rosa Parks had to agree to go to court that Monday, December 5, for her trial. Then she and her husband and their friends went back to the Parkses' house to figure out what to do next.

CHAPTER 6

Ain't Gonna Ride That Bus No More

Segregation on public transportation in the South

Why was sitting in the back of the bus a big deal?

It was a daily humiliation. Black people couldn't even go to work or school without being reminded that they were second-class citizens. And it was hard to avoid the buses, because most people couldn't afford cars.

❝ Whites would accuse you of causing trouble when all you were doing was acting like a normal human being instead of cringing. You didn't have to wait for a lynching. You died a little each time you found yourself face to face with this kind of discrimination. The question of where we had to sit on the bus wasn't a little thing. It was painful to get on a bus and have to pass by all those empty seats up front in order to stand in the rear. The most painful thing of all was to see little children on the bus. To them a seat was a seat and when they saw an empty one, they sat down. Their mothers would have to snatch them up and hurry them to the rear before there was trouble. It was painful to think of how they would be taught. They would have to stand in the back just because of their color. **❞**

—**Rosa Parks** in *Black Profiles,* 1970

How fast did E. D. Nixon ask Rosa to be a test case for the Supreme Court?

Practically as soon as they got back to her house.

Parks kept saying, "Rosa, they'll kill you." He had worried for a long time that his wife's political work was dangerous. Rosa knew that she would be putting herself and her family in danger. She knew she'd lose her job for being a "troublemaker," and she made more money than Parks, who'd been missing work at the air force base barbershop because of illness. She also knew that what E. D. Nixon was saying was right: Hers was the perfect case. Unlike the other women arrested, Rosa Parks was not charged with disturbing the peace—only with breaking the segregation law. "The white people couldn't point to me and say there was anything I had done to deserve such treatment except to be born black," Rosa Parks later wrote. Her husband and mother agreed, but they weren't happy about it. Neither was she, since she didn't like being the center of attention. But she knew it was the right thing to do.

How long did it take the black community of Montgomery to plan the Supreme Court case and the bus boycott?

One night—and if you think that means some people didn't get much sleep, you're right.

The NAACP Legal Defense and Education Fund had to help with money, because taking a case all the way to the Supreme Court is expensive. Thurgood Marshall was still in charge of the fund, and Clifford Durr was sure Marshall would help. Fred Gray would be Rosa's lawyer.

After Gray received a phone call from Nixon, he called Jo Ann Robinson, the WPC president who had written a letter to the mayor threatening a bus boycott. Professor Robinson immediately called some members of the WPC, and they agreed that the moment had come. She later wrote, "We had planned the protest long before Mrs. Parks was arrested. There had been so many things that happened, that black women had been embarrassed over, and they were ready to explode."

In the middle of the night, Jo Ann Robinson had a night watchman let her into the college where she taught. She made thirty-five thousand copies of a flyer announcing a one-day bus boycott on Monday—a time-consuming process, especially in the days before photocopy machines. At three o'clock in the morning, she called E. D. Nixon to let him know what she was doing. (She was afraid she'd wake him up, but he was already awake.) By morning, she and her students and WPC members were ready to deliver the flyers to houses, schools, stores, bars, and churches. By evening almost every black person in Montgomery knew about the boycott.

> ### "PLEASE STAY OFF OF ALL BUSES MONDAY":
> #### JO ANN ROBINSON'S ANNOUNCEMENT OF THE BUS BOYCOTT
>
> This is for Monday, December 5, 1955
>
> Another Negro woman has been arrested and thrown in jail because she refused to get up out of her seat on the bus for a white person to sit down.
>
> It is the second time since the Claudette Colvin case that a Negro woman has been arrested for the same thing. This has to be stopped.
>
> Negroes have rights, too, for if Negroes did not ride the buses, they could not operate. Three-fourths of the riders are Negroes, yet we are arrested, or have to stand over empty seats. If we do not do something to stop these arrests, they will continue. The next time it may be you, or your daughter, or mother.
>
> This woman's case will come up Monday. We are, therefore, asking every Negro to stay off the buses Monday in protest of the arrest and trial. Don't ride the buses to work, to town, to school, or anywhere on Monday.
>
> You can afford to stay out of school for one day if you have no other way to go except by bus.
>
> You can also afford to stay out of town for one day. If you work, take a cab, or walk. But please, children and grown-ups, don't ride the bus at all on Monday. Please stay off of all buses Monday.

Why did the churches become so important in the Civil Rights movement?

Jo Ann Robinson and the WPC really organized the boycott, but the way to best communicate with the black community of Montgomery was through its churches. A church was also the only place large numbers of blacks could meet legally, and there were going to be some really big meetings. After the Monday boycott, there was going to be a meeting to decide if it had worked and if people should keep boycotting.

E. D. Nixon called Reverend Ralph David Abernathy, whom he knew from the NAACP. Reverend Abernathy called Reverend Martin Luther King Jr. and some other ministers. He told them what had happened to Rosa Parks and explained about the bus boycott for Monday.

Besides spreading the word through churches, Nixon called a white newspaper reporter, Joe Azbell, who supported Civil Rights. Nixon said that he had the hottest story in town. He knew that a newspaper article about the boycott would get the news to even more people.

What did Rosa Parks do the day after she was arrested?

Rosa Parks went to work on Friday, but she took a taxi. She wasn't going to wait until Monday for the boycott to begin. She had already decided she was never again going to sit on a segregated bus.

Her boss was shocked to see her. He thought she'd be a "nervous wreck." Rosa Parks replied, "Why should going to jail make a nervous wreck out of me?" During her lunch break, she went to visit Fred Gray in his usually quiet office, as she often did. The phones didn't stop ringing that day. People were calling or stopping by to find out about the boycott.

But still, no one could be sure the boycott would work. Suppose it rained? Suppose people couldn't figure out how to get to work? Suppose people got hurt?

Rosa Parks worried—and prayed.

Did people ride the bus on Monday?

No. Nearly all the buses were empty of black people. Kids chased the buses, yelling, "No riders today!" The boycott was almost a 100 percent success.

"We surprised ourselves," said E. D. Nixon.

Where were the black people of Montgomery on Monday?

Rosa and Raymond Parks went to the courthouse. Rosa Parks wore her most ladylike clothes: a black dress with white cuffs, a little black velvet hat with pearl trim, and white gloves. She was so sure that she was doing the right thing that she wasn't even very nervous. The fact that Rosa Parks dressed like a lady and looked calm wasn't unexpected. She'd been doing that since her grandfather brought her to the doctor when she was a little girl. The surprise was how many black people were waiting at the courthouse.

The courtroom was so crowded that Raymond Parks had to identify himself to get in. Hundreds of supporters surrounded the courthouse, including teens from the NAACP Youth Council. One of them, Mary Frances, shouted, "Oh, she's so sweet. They've messed with the wrong one now."

"They've messed with the wrong one now" was what everyone said after that, and they said it over and over again. Rosa Parks knew what it meant. Everything she had learned from her mother, grandparents, her church, Miss White's school, her husband, the NAACP, and Highlander Folk School made Rosa Parks the wrong one to mess with and the *right* person to unite Montgomery's black community in a boycott.

Although Rosa Parks usually hated being the center of attention, she wasn't embarrassed when all the people showed up at the courthouse. She welcomed them. Later she wrote, "The one thing I appreciated was the fact that when so many others, by the hundreds and by the thousands, joined in, there was a kind of lifting of a burden from me individually. I could feel that whatever my individual desires were to be free, I was not alone. There were many others who felt the same way."

When is a "guilty" verdict a good thing?

The court took only thirty minutes to convict Rosa Parks of breaking the segregation laws. She was fined fourteen dollars, more than half of her weekly salary. It wasn't bad news. Fred Gray and Montgomery's other black lawyer, Charles Langford, needed her to be found guilty so they could bring the case all the way to the U.S. Supreme Court. Everyone involved with the case understood that.

Did people decide to continue the boycott?

Rosa Parks could barely get to the church where the Monday night meeting was being held. The meeting was at 7 p.m., but by 5 p.m. the Holt Street Baptist Church was already overflowing—and this was the biggest church in the city. Cars were parked all over the sidewalks and lawns. About five thousand people had come. Loudspeakers had to be put up so that everyone outside could hear the meeting.

Some of the meeting's organizers thought there would be just the one-day boycott. Then maybe a committee would go to the bus company and ask them again to negotiate, now that the city had seen what a boycott could do. But the huge number of people who had stayed off the buses and who came to this December 5 meeting showed that the ordinary, tired black people of Montgomery were ready to fight for change.

66 You who are afraid, you better get your hat and coat and go home. I want to tell you something: For years and years I've been talking about how I didn't want the children who came along behind me to suffer the indignities that I've suffered all these years. Well, I've changed my mind—I want to enjoy some of that freedom myself. 99

—**E. D. Nixon**, speaking at the Monday night meeting, December 5, 1955

What was the Montgomery Improvement Association?

During the day of December 5, a group of ministers and community leaders had formed an organization to run the boycott. They called it the Montgomery Improvement Association (MIA), and asked Martin Luther King Jr. to lead it. There were a lot of black organizations in Montgomery, but there had never been one that everyone could belong to. The NAACP was made up of mostly educated men. The WPC was middle-class and professional women. Various black ministers held sway over different groups. One man owned a nightclub that only registered voters could belong to.

The formation of the MIA—an organization for *everyone* who wanted to be part of the boycott—was important. Most people hadn't believed that the blacks of Montgomery could all work together. Mary Fair Burks (the founder of the WPC) had seen the problem the day she gave out the bus boycott flyers. She had to explain the flyer to some people because they couldn't read. Then she went to a big card party given for middle-class black ladies of Montgomery.

But all these people—the ones who couldn't read and the ones who attended fancy parties, the bricklayers and the business owners—were going to have to work together. People from all these groups knew and trusted Rosa Parks. She worked as a seamstress, was married to a barber, and never had much money—but she was also an educated lady who had worked with the NAACP.

Did Martin Luther King Jr. become president of the MIA because he was so famous?

Dr. Martin Luther King Jr.

The ministers and black leaders in Montgomery didn't all agree with or even like one another. But Dr. King hadn't been around Montgomery long enough to annoy anyone, as E. D. Nixon and some other leaders had. He didn't belong to any of the groups that were fighting about who would get to be in charge—so he was elected president in the hope that he would help unite everyone. He got elected because he *wasn't* famous. And, although the newspapers called Dr. King the boycott's leader, in many ways it didn't have one. Later, when a judge asked Claudette Colvin who their leaders were, she said, "Our leaders is just we ourselves."

How long did it take Dr. King to write his speech for the Monday night meeting?

Dr. King usually spent about fifteen hours writing out every word of his Sunday sermons. But he'd been so busy that he'd only had twenty minutes to prepare his speech for the Monday meeting, so that night he had to speak mostly from his heart. To his surprise, it was the best speech he had ever given. After he spoke, it was clear that something very important was happening in Montgomery. People interrupted King to cheer and shout "Amen" and "That's right." When he was done speaking, people stood up and clapped and cheered for fifteen minutes. As one newspaper reporter said, people were "on fire for freedom."

" My friends, I want it to be known that we're going to work with grim and firm determination to gain justice on the buses in this city. And we are not wrong, we are not wrong in what we are doing. If we are wrong, then the Constitution of the United States is wrong. If we are wrong, God Almighty is wrong. . . . If we are wrong, justice is a lie. And we are determined in Montgomery to work and fight until justice runs down like water and righteousness like a mighty stream. . . . "

—The Reverend Dr. **Martin Luther King Jr.**, December 5, 1955

Did Rosa Parks speak at the meeting?

No, although she was sitting with the leaders. One of the ministers introduced her to the crowd, who chanted her name and yelled, "Thank you, sister." People told her, "You have done enough and you have said enough and you don't have to speak."

Reverend Abernathy said later, "Mrs. Rosa Parks was presented to the mass meeting because we wanted her to become symbolic of our protest movement." He later called her an "adornment"—a decoration— to the movement. The story of Rosa Parks as that nice tired seamstress seems to begin here, with male leaders who talk about her as a symbol rather than as a trained and experienced Civil Rights worker. In truth, she was both: a trained Civil Rights leader *and* someone who became a symbol. She was someone people could hold in their hearts to remind them to be brave, a real person who would remind them of what they were fighting for. The

New York Times called her a "Negro seamstress," but for many protesters she was "an angel walking."

THE MOTHER OF THE CIVIL RIGHTS MOVEMENT?

Many people, black and white, have fought for the rights of black people ever since slaves were first brought to this continent in 1619. After slavery was outlawed, people continued to work for these rights. That's what the NAACP was doing, and their work led to the Supreme Court decision about school desegregation. Other people had been arrested in protests. But when people talk nowadays about the Civil Rights movement, they usually mean the protests of the 1950s and 1960s that began with the bus boycott in Montgomery. People call Rosa Parks "the mother of the Civil Rights movement" because when she refused to give up her seat, something new was born.

Rosa Parks says that it's important for people to know that she was just one of the people who has worked for change. But she has also said, "It's all right if that's what people want to call me. Things have been said about me that were not so complimentary."

AMERICAN VOICES

❝ The fear that had shackled us all across the years left us suddenly when we were in that church together. ❞
—Rev. **Ralph Abernathy**, writing about the Monday night meeting

Was the MIA demanding an end to segregation on the buses?

After Dr. King spoke, Reverend Abernathy read the list of changes that the bus company would have to make before the boycott would end. You might think they'd be asking for an end to segregation, but they weren't. Segregation wasn't the bus company's rule; it was the state law. The bus company couldn't end segregation. The court case would have to do that. The MIA demanded three things from the bus company:

1. Drivers must treat passengers politely.

2. There must be new rules for seating. Black people would first fill seats in the back of the bus, and whites sit in the front, but black people wouldn't have to give up their seats to whites.

3. The bus company must hire some black drivers.

Did everyone want to continue the boycott?

YES! (And that's what they said.)

What did the bus company and the city council say about the boycotters' demands?

They said that the drivers weren't rude to black riders. They said they wouldn't hire black drivers. (Well, maybe, they said—in about ten years.) And they said that the boycotters' plan for seating broke state law, because it wasn't segregated enough. Lawyer Fred Gray said that it couldn't possibly be against state law, because the city of Mobile, Alabama, already used that seating plan. But the city commissioner said, "If we grant the Negroes these demands, they would go about boasting of a victory that they had won over the white people, and this we will not stand for."

CHAPTER 7

The Walking City

An editorial cartoon published in the *Washington Post*,
March 25, 1956

How did people get around the city during the boycott?

People walked everywhere in all kinds of weather: in the sun and in the rain, going to school or going to work, or all dressed up for church. Many were happy, striding along. Many were tired.

But people were proud to walk. "I wanted to be one of them that tried to make it better," said a woman named Gussie Nesbitt. One old woman who was offered a ride said, "I'm not walking for myself. I'm walking for my children and my grandchildren." People like these had grumbled when Rosa Parks wouldn't enter the bus by the back steps, and they didn't help when she was arrested. They had thought they couldn't do anything to show whites how tired they were of being pushed around. Now they *could* show them: They could walk. This is how Montgomery got to be called "The Walking City."

Did everyone walk all the time?

Some did, but there were other ways of getting around as well. Many white women would give rides to the black women who worked as their housekeepers and cooks. When the mayor complained that these white women were helping the boycott succeed, some of them said they'd quit driving their maids and nannies and cooks when the mayor showed up himself to wash their dishes and clean their houses. Some of those women just didn't want to wash dishes. Others said they were glad to help the black community protest segregation, and they gave money to the MIA.

Before the boycott more than thirty thousand black people rode the buses to work and back every day. Now they were walking and riding bicycles. Some people rode mules or drove horses and buggies. The MIA kept coming up with ways to get people around the city, and the police and city government kept shutting them down.

When the black cab companies offered rides for ten cents (the same price as a bus ride), city officials arrested the drivers for offering illegally low fares.

When blacks (and a few whites) who owned cars gave rides to anyone who needed them, charging fifteen cents for gas, the police said they were running an illegal taxi company.

The MIA finally invented its own free public transportation system. People lent them cars, and the churches bought station wagons. The congregation members would say with pride, "There goes my church" when a car with their church's name on it rolled by. Many people—including Jo Ann Robinson and several ministers—volunteered to be drivers. One elegant old black woman, who was usually chauffeured by her own private driver, took her big green Cadillac out every morning and gave rides to the workmen and storekeepers and cooks trying to get to their jobs. The MIA made a huge schedule of pick-up and drop-off times and places all over the city. Rosa Parks and other MIA volunteers worked as dispatchers, sending cars for people who needed rides at other times. Sometimes Rosa would work from five-thirty in the morning until midnight. Everyone—black and white—was amazed how well the system worked.

❝ Ain't gonna ride them buses no more,

Ain't gonna ride no more.

Why don't all the white folks know

That I ain't gonna ride no more. ❞

—A song sung by Montgomery bus boycotters

How did the city commissioners try to trick the boycotters?

In January 1956 they made a deal with three ministers who weren't part of the MIA. They agreed to change the bus seating a little and add some all-black buses, but that's all. Then the city commissioners announced in the Saturday *Montgomery Advertiser* that the boycott was over. But Dr. King found out the news and asked all the MIA ministers to tell people to keep walking.

When the boycott continued, the city commissioners lost their tempers, because they looked like fools. The mayor and the top government officials joined the local White Citizens' Council. The mayor said it was time to "get tough" with the boycotters.

AMERICAN VOICES

❝ White people do not care whether Negroes ever ride the buses again. We are not going to be a part of any program that will get Negroes to ride buses again at the [cost of the] destruction of our heritage and way of life. ❞

—**Mayor Gayle**, January 23, 1956

Did Rosa Parks think being a hero was fun?

Some people she worked with at Montgomery Fair stopped talking to her. Then her boss told her that the store's tailor shop was being closed, so they didn't need her anymore. Rosa Parks started taking in sewing at home and continued to volunteer many hours working for the boycott. Raymond Parks quit his job as a barber on the Maxwell air force base. His white boss said that no mention of the boycott or of Rosa Parks would be allowed. Parks said he couldn't work in a place where he wasn't allowed to say the name of his own wife.

Death threats began to arrive by phone and mail. Their rent was raised. Without a job, Raymond Parks stayed home and worried so much about his wife's safety that he started drinking and smoking too much. Rosa's mother was scared too. She would pick up the phone and hear cursing.

Was Rosa Parks frightened by these threats?

Naturally she was frightened, but not in a way that made her want to stop working for Civil Rights—and at times she stopped being afraid altogether. "Well, you have to die sometime," she said at one point. "[If] they killed me, then I would just be dead." She did worry about her family's safety.

Martin Luther King Jr. was more frightened. He was a young man—twenty-six years old—with a wife and a baby girl. He hadn't been a Civil Rights worker for thirteen years like Rosa Parks had. One time he was so frightened that he cried. Dr. King prayed that God would make him strong and tell him what to do. He later said that he heard "an inner voice" tell him to "Stand up for righteousness. Stand up for justice. Stand up for truth." He wasn't afraid anymore, even though dynamite was thrown at his house three days later, destroying his front porch and windows.

WHOSE SIDE WAS GOD ON?

Rosa Parks also said God was with her, but the segregationists believed God was on their side. Ministers fought both for and against desegregation.

At one time or another, Christians, Jews, Muslims, Hindus, and followers of other religions have said that God wanted them to kill their enemies. In a war both sides pray to God. Terrorists, including the KKK, often say they are doing what God wants.

Trust in God helped Rosa Parks and many other people work peacefully, patiently, and steadily for Civil Rights. It's not possible to understand how Rosa Parks has lived without understanding that religion has always guided and strengthened her. However, others have worked as steadily for justice without believing in God.

What made segregationists even angrier?

On January 31, 1956, Fred Gray filed the lawsuit saying that bus segregation was unconstitutional. He and lawyer Charles Langford got ready to argue before the U.S. Supreme Court that if segregation in schools was unconstitutional, so was segregation on the buses. The MIA and the NAACP had been waiting for the right time to begin the court case. They didn't really just want more polite segregation on the buses—they wanted no segregation anywhere.

Segregationists reacted to news of the lawsuit with more violence. Someone threw a bomb at E. D. Nixon's house. Rosa Parks helped clean up the mess. White students at the University of Alabama rioted when the first black student, Autherine Lucy, was admitted in 1956. As tensions in the city grew, ten thousand whites attended a white supremacy rally in Montgomery. Flying Confederate flags, they bragged that they'd give blacks a "whipping" and "teach Rosa Parks a 'harsh lesson.'" Segregationists destroyed cars belonging to black people, sprayed their gardens with poison to kill the plants, and threw rotten eggs and bricks at black people walking.

One black neighborhood in Montgomery was bombed so often that it was nicknamed "Dynamite Hill." Whites who publicly supported the boycott had their houses bombed too. The Parks residence was never bombed.

NONVIOLENCE AND THE CIVIL RIGHTS MOVEMENT

During the boycott, if the black people of Montgomery had fought back when white people threw things and cursed them, there would have been riots and lynchings. But Dr. King said that Jesus preached loving your enemies and "turning the other cheek"—not fighting back even when attacked. Dr. King had learned about nonviolent political protests from the writings of Mahatma Gandhi, a Hindu. Gandhi taught the people of India to use peaceful protest, and together they'd freed their country from Great Britain. Bayard Rustin, the American Civil Rights worker who was arrested for his earlier peaceful "freedom rides," went to Montgomery to teach everyone how to run a nonviolent protest. For instance, he told Dr. King to get all the guns out of his house!

Politically active high school and college students also began to learn how to protest nonviolently. They practiced standing or sitting quietly while people threw things at them, called them names, and hit them. Not all of them were religious, but they had learned that nonviolent protests worked.

What was the "dumbest act that had ever been done in Montgomery"?

Soon after the supremacy rally, the city accused 115 people, including Rosa Parks, Dr. King, Abernathy, Nixon, and twenty-four ministers, of breaking an old law that made boycotts illegal. When Rosa Parks heard about this, she didn't wait for the police to come get her. She and many others dressed in their best clothes and took themselves proudly and angrily to the courthouse to be arrested. A total of 87 protestors were arrested. People who weren't on the list complained.

This time, Rosa Parks took herself to the courthouse to be arrested.

Editor Grover Hall Jr. wrote in the *Montgomery Advertiser* that this was the dumbest thing the city of Montgomery could have done. The boycott was now front-page news across the country. "The Negroes are not on trial here," preached one minister. "Montgomery is on trial." Thousands of dollars of contributions poured in. The NAACP promised to send lawyers to defend everyone. So many people made fun of Montgomery that the city dropped the cases against everyone except King, who was fined five hundred dollars (or 386 days of hard labor). Many whites in the city were glad. A group of white businessmen calling themselves the Men of Montgomery were trying to get the mayor to settle the boycott. The loss of business caused by the boycott meant that their stores were going broke. And they didn't like that their city was behaving badly while the whole world was watching.

What did people send to Montgomery?

When people heard about the boycott, they sent lots of shoes! Many people were wearing their shoes out walking to work or school. Others needed shoes, as well as clothes, food, and money, because they'd lost their jobs. Many of the donations were sent directly to Rosa Parks. One of her jobs during this time was getting donations to the people who needed them most.

What else was Rosa Parks doing to help the boycott?

Schools, churches, and NAACP groups all over the country wanted her to come and talk about her arrest and about what the black people of Montgomery were doing.

In May 1956 she flew to New York City and spoke at Madison Square Garden about Civil Rights. Then she spent two weeks in New York City, meeting some of her heroes, including Roy Wilkins, the national head of the NAACP, and Eleanor Roosevelt, the former first lady. People took her picture and asked for her autograph.

Did Rosa Parks get rich making speeches all over the country?

Often the people she spoke to could pay only her expenses, but not any extra. If she collected money, it went toward the boycott. So when Rosa Parks got back to Montgomery, she was in debt. No one in her family was earning any money, and the MIA had not given her a paid secretarial job.

She was also tired and ill. She had liked seeing the country but hadn't liked being so far from home.

Was Raymond Parks excited about the boycott?

We don't know very much about Raymond Parks during this time, because he and his wife wished to keep their lives private. He had been one of Rosa Parks's most important teachers about Civil Rights, but by the time the boycott started, he seems to have fallen apart. He was afraid and drinking too much. Yet Rosa Parks speaks and writes of her husband only with love and respect. She once admitted that her hair, which rippled all the way down her back when loose, was hard to take care of—but she kept it that way because her husband liked it long. Perhaps we can only know that the boycott was a hard time for Raymond Parks, but that he and his wife loved each other very much.

What finally happened with the court case against Montgomery's bus segregation?

On June 5, 1956, the U.S. District Court (the state branch of the United States federal court) said that segregated seating laws were unconstitutional. This was good news, but it wasn't time to stop the boycott yet. As the MIA expected, the State of Alabama asked the United States Supreme Court to hear the case, hoping for a different decision. The blacks in Montgomery kept walking.

On November 13 the United States Supreme Court ruled 9 to 0 in support of the district court's ruling.

The court had wanted total agreement, and they got it. They were going down in history saying that "separate and equal" was wrong, because separate wasn't equal, not in schools, not on buses, not anywhere. Their decision told the boycotters and the NAACP lawyers that this court would find other cases of segregation of public facilities—such as trains, waiting rooms, and water fountains—illegal.

On December 20, 1956, the Supreme Court delivered its order to desegregate the buses: a real order, in writing. After more than a year, the boycott was over.

What did Montgomery segregationists do about the ruling?

The Ku Klux Klan marched and drove through black neighborhoods. Usually this made black people go into their houses and lock the doors. This time people stood on the sidewalks and porches—and laughed.

But segregationists still bombed black churches and MIA ministers' houses. They shot at the buses. A pregnant black woman was shot in the legs. For a time the city refused to run any buses at all.

Yet by the end of January, integrated buses were running on a normal schedule.

Was the Supreme Court decision a real victory?

"Many whites, even white Southerners, told me that even though it may have seemed like the blacks were being freed, they felt more free and at ease themselves," Rosa Parks said after the boycott was over. And yet, she explained, "It didn't feel like a victory, actually. There was still a great deal to do." Many Southern schools were refusing to integrate. Blacks still could not register to vote. But the buses of Montgomery were integrated, and other cities were suing to desegregate their own bus systems. Some people, including some members of the NAACP, said the boycott hadn't mattered—that the court case, not the boycott, changed the laws. But the boycott mattered to the black people of Montgomery. In other cities, even after the buses were desegregated, black people still went to the back of the bus. In Montgomery black people sat wherever they wanted. They felt they had earned that right for themselves.

Ordinary people had learned that peaceful protests could make a difference. For the next ten years, nonviolent "direct action" protests—boycotts, marches, and other public acts—would be important tools of the Civil Rights movement.

CHAPTER 8

Quiet Strength

Rosa Parks was honored on her seventy-fifth birthday in Detroit.

Why did Rosa Parks move to Detroit?

Rosa Parks continued to get hostile phone calls, and she was threatened on the street. She began to think that someone might really kill her. Raymond Parks was sick with fear. He began sleeping with a gun near him. No one would give either of them a job. Rosa Parks was known in white Montgomery as a "troublemaker."

Dr. King was considered the leader of the bus boycott and of the Civil Rights movement. When newspaper reporters and photographers came to take pictures of the Civil Rights leaders on the first integrated buses, they didn't even include Rosa Parks. She was home with her mother, who was ill. Later that day some people from *Look* magazine did come and take photographs of her on a bus—one that James Blake was driving, which neither of them enjoyed. But it was King who was now big news, and in January 1957 a group of black Baptist preachers made him president of a new Civil Rights group, the Southern Christian Leadership Conference (SCLC).

Not even all Rosa Parks's friends were supportive; many people from the MIA—like Nixon and Reverend Abernathy—were jealous. A lot of people had worked hard for the boycott, but the newspapers paid attention mostly to Rosa Parks (as a saint, or at least as a symbol of courage) and to Martin Luther King Jr. (as a leader). It's said that some of the Baptist ministers greeted her with, "Well! If it isn't the superstar!" She was horrified, and hurt.

Her friends—and the black community in general—were ashamed of themselves when they heard that Rosa Parks and her family would be moving to begin again in Detroit, near Sylvester McCauley and his family. They sent them off with a party and eight hundred dollars.

Did Rosa Parks ever go to college?

In Detroit she joined the local NAACP but immediately began traveling again, speaking about Civil Rights and the boycott. The president of Hampton Institute in Virginia, where Booker T.

Washington had studied, heard Rosa's speech, and he offered her a job. She worked as the hostess of the college's guest and residence house for a year in 1958. Although she wasn't studying there, she still liked working on a college campus, being around black college students and supervising people.

She hoped that her family would be able to join her in Virginia, but that wasn't possible. She couldn't find an apartment for them or a job for Parks, who was now working at a barbering college back in Detroit.

What did Rosa do when she got back to Detroit?

She continued to do volunteer work for Civil Rights and in the church. She still traveled and gave speeches about the bus boycott. But to earn money, she made aprons in a small clothing factory. While working there she met sixteen-year-old Elaine Easton Steele. Elaine could hardly believe she was sewing aprons with the famous Rosa Parks. Their boss could hardly believe that a girl could talk as much and sew as slowly as Elaine did, and he fired her—but not before Rosa and Elaine became friends.

WHEN COULD TRYING TO BUY A HAMBURGER GET YOU THROWN IN JAIL?

When Rosa Parks said, "There was still a great deal to do," she was right. Southern states continued to fight integration. Many schools remained segregated, even after the 1954 ruling by the Supreme Court. In 1957 President Eisenhower had been forced to call in the National Guard when the governor of Arkansas used state troopers to keep nine black students out of all-white Little Rock Central High School.

High school and college students were becoming more and more important to the Civil Rights movement. In the early 1960s, students—black and white—began to have "sit-ins" at lunch counters that refused to serve blacks. Trained in nonviolent political action, the students remained quiet while they were cursed, beaten, covered with ketchup, burned with cigarettes, and jailed. (The people who beat them were not jailed.) A few months later, stores began to integrate their lunch counters. "Lie-ins" (at segregated hotels) and "wade-ins" (at segregated swimming pools) soon followed.

Did Rosa Parks hear Dr. King's famous "I have a dream" speech?

Yes—twice. Martin Luther King Jr. gave his most famous speech at an August 28, 1963, march on Washington, D.C., to a crowd of 250,000 people. But he did a dress rehearsal in Detroit first, and Rosa Parks was at his side. She loved that speech and bought a record of it to play over and over again. But in some ways she didn't like the march itself because she and Septima Clark and the other women Civil Rights workers were not allowed to speak or even to march with the men. "Nowadays, women wouldn't stand for being kept so much in the background," Rosa Parks wrote later, "but back then, women's rights hadn't become a popular cause yet."

66 My life-time mission has been simple, that all men and women are created equal under the eyes of our Lord. **99**

—**Rosa Parks** to Pope John Paul II, in a letter after they met in 1993

How did Rosa Parks get a job working for a congressman?

John Conyers was a black lawyer who ran for the U.S. House of Representatives in 1964 with the slogan, "Jobs, Justice, Peace."

Rosa Parks worked in his office as a volunteer while he campaigned. She also got Martin Luther King Jr. to endorse him in a speech. It was the only time anyone convinced Dr. King to endorse a candidate. Congressman Conyers believed that King's speech got him elected, and he knew Rosa Parks had made it happen. Nearly the first thing he did when he was elected was to hire her to work for him—for pay—in his office in Detroit. He said that people used to come to his office to meet her, not him!

Some people weren't happy with Rosa Parks's new position. Soon after she was hired, they sent her death threats. They said she was a troublemaker and shouldn't be working for Conyers—she should be cleaning someone's house. But Conyers noticed that she would never say a bad word about anyone and would never ever get into an argument. He also noticed that she was stubborn when she believed she was right.

What was "Bloody Sunday"?

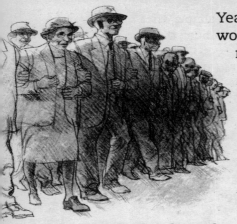

Years after Rosa Parks began working for voter registration, Southern blacks were still prevented from voting. In 1964 President Lyndon Johnson had signed the Civil Rights Act, but most blacks still were prevented from voting. So they marched. On Sunday, March 7, 1965, hundreds of people—mostly black and some white—began to march the fifty miles from Selma, Alabama, to the state capitol building in Montgomery. Rosa Parks saw what happened on television: State troopers stopped the march six blocks from its starting point. They attacked marchers with tear gas, electric cattle prods, and clubs. Rosa Parks knew some of the people being attacked.

When Martin Luther King Jr. asked her to be in another Selma-to-Montgomery march on March 21, she went. It was an odd experience. Montgomery felt like home to her, but she was fifty-two and the younger people didn't recognize her. After all, she had been away for six years. People leading the last part of the march were supposed to be wearing special jackets, and Rosa Parks didn't have one. Organizers would pull her out of the march, and then someone would recognize her and pull her back in. At the end she was in front with Martin

Luther King Jr., Roy Wilkins, and other Civil Rights leaders. No one was hurt in this march, and they reached Montgomery on March 25. A few months later, on August 8, Johnson signed the Voting Rights Act. This law worked, because it said that if Southerners wouldn't register people to vote, then the U.S. government would send the military to do it. Finally blacks were able to vote in the South—one hundred years after the slaves were freed.

Why was the Voting Rights Act followed by rioting?

Things were changing, but slowly—too slowly for some people. Civil Rights workers might have been nonviolent at first, but that didn't keep the Klan—or the police—from killing them. In the cities rage was building up among young black men and women, from too many years of injustice.

On August 13 a black driver was arrested by a white police officer in a section of Los Angeles called Watts—and the city exploded in six days of race riots. It became a bloody war zone, in which thirty-four people were killed and $200 million dollars of property damage was caused. In the summers that followed, other cities—including Detroit—burned in riots. The Civil Rights movement as Rosa Parks had known it was finished, fractured into different groups with different beliefs about how to get justice and equality for black citizens of America.

What did Rosa Parks think when the Civil Rights movement stopped being dedicated to nonviolence?

Rosa Parks said that the Civil Rights movement would never have succeeded except by nonviolence.

Yet she also said, "I was raised to be proud, and it had worked for me to stand up aggressively for myself." When she was growing up, she had found that threatening someone with a brick was sometimes necessary, and she never really changed her mind about that.

But the Detroit race riots of 1967 angered and frightened her. For days Rosa and Raymond Parks couldn't eat, work, or sleep. They looked out from their apartment window and saw the stores they shopped in being burned and looted. Parks's barbershop was looted, and their car was destroyed. Rosa Parks was concerned that looters and thieves made the Civil Rights movement look bad.

How had Rosa Parks's views changed in the 1960s?

Rosa Parks admired some of America's young black political leaders who disagreed with Martin Luther King Jr. Although she had worked for integration, she hadn't wanted to go to the bus company with a piece of paper asking the "white folks" for favors. In the 1960s the new black political leaders like Malcolm X were tired of asking for favors too—even favors like being allowed to eat at a white lunch counter.

Rosa Parks, who had always been prim and white gloved, began to sometimes wear more clothes in African styles made of African fabrics, and she went to rallies for America's first all-black political party. She didn't approve of anyone preaching hatred of whites, but she also wanted blacks to know more about their own history and culture.

What was the hardest time for Rosa Parks?

When Martin Luther King Jr. was assassinated in Memphis, Tennessee, on April 4, 1968, Rosa Parks said, "I was lost. How else can I describe it?"

Two months after Dr. King's death, Senator Robert Kennedy, a strong supporter of Civil Rights, was shot. His brother President John F. Kennedy and Malcolm X had already been killed. The dream of a peaceful Civil Rights movement died with them, in a decade of assassinations and riots. "It seemed like we were losing everybody we thought was good," Rosa Parks said.

In the early 1970s, Rosa Parks's husband, mother, and brother were all sick. For a while Rosa Parks spent her days traveling from hospital to hospital to see them. Raymond Parks died in 1977, after a five-year illness, and Sylvester McCauley died three months later. Leona McCauley died in 1979. Through much of this time, Rosa Parks had been sick or injured herself, suffering everything from ulcers to a broken ankle. She had been photographed so many times that the flashbulbs had damaged her eyes. Still she tried to answer her own mail—thousands and thousands of letters.

Who reappeared in Rosa Parks's life to help her out?

Rosa Parks and Elaine Steele—the girl in the apron factory who liked to talk—more or less adopted each other. They both worked in Detroit's federal building, where Rosa Parks assisted Congressman Conyers and Elaine Steele had a job in the court. Rosa Parks had often given Elaine Steele a ride to work. Now a married woman with children, Elaine Steele started to accompany Rosa Parks on speaking trips around the country, and generally tried to say no when Rosa Parks couldn't.

In 1987 Elaine Steele also helped her found the Rosa and Raymond Parks Institute for Self-Development. Rosa Parks wanted to teach teens what she was learning about black culture, what she'd learned at Highlander about Civil Rights, and what she'd learned from her mother and at Miss White's— "hope, dignity, and pride." She told them to listen to the stories that their parents and grandparents and old people tell, to learn their history. Rosa Parks took teens on bus tours to the places on the Underground Railroad. Some of those teens had never been out of Detroit. While they were traveling, the rules were a little like a modern version of Miss White's: no smoking, no video games—and lectures from Rosa Parks about eating their vegetables and writing in their journals. She wanted black teenagers to be healthy, well educated, brave, free, and proud.

Did a black leader from South Africa know about Rosa Parks?

WHAT DOES IT MEAN?

Apartheid is South Africa's word for the legalized segregation of blacks and whites, which was ended in 1991.

Nelson Mandela, who would become the president of South Africa in 1994, had spent twenty-seven years in jail for his peaceful fight against *apartheid*. Elaine Steele arranged for Rosa Parks to be there when his plane landed in Detroit during a 1990 visit after his release from prison. Rosa Parks admired him very

much, but she didn't think he'd know who she was. When a friend shoved her in front of the crowds, she was embarrassed. Crowds of people began chanting Mandela's name when he got off the plane, but he walked right up to Rosa and started a chant of his own: "Ro-sa Parks. Ro-sa Parks." Then they hugged each other, like family. He knew exactly who she was.

Later Mandela would say, "Before King there was Rosa Parks. She is who inspired us, who taught us to sit down for our rights, to be fearless when facing our oppressors."

What was Rosa Parks's least favorite time she was in the news?

In 1994, as she was getting ready for bed, Rosa Parks heard a loud noise downstairs. When she investigated, she found a young black man who smelled like whiskey. He claimed to have scared away a burglar, and he asked for a few dollars. Rosa Parks went upstairs to get her purse, and he followed her. Then he said he wanted *all* her money.

Being Rosa Parks, she told him, "No. That's not right." The robber beat her until she at last told him to take the money. Then she called Elaine Steele, who called the police and ambulance.

Friends, newspaper columnists, and political leaders had a fit: A city or country that couldn't protect "the mother of the Civil Rights movement" was in big trouble. Rosa Parks herself worried that people would think badly of all young black men, because of what one man had done. She also moved to an apartment building that had a security guard.

How has Rosa Parks been honored?

The city of Montgomery has honored Rosa Parks in many ways. They renamed the street she lived on during the boycott Rosa L. Parks Boulevard and invited her to be an honored guest when the Civil Rights memorial was dedicated in 1989. Montgomery's Troy University opened a Rosa Parks Museum in 2000, right next to the place where she refused to give up her seat. Multimedia exhibits tell the story of the bus boycott and include a replica of the bus.

WHERE IS THAT BUS PARKED NOW?

After rusting in a field for thirty years, Rosa Parks's famous bus was auctioned on the Internet in 2001. The bus, which cost almost half a million dollars to restore, is now displayed in the Henry Ford Museum in Dearborn, Michigan.

Rosa Parks has been honored in many other ways over the years. Her seventy-seventh birthday was celebrated on television in 1990. President Clinton awarded her the Presidential Medal of Freedom in 1996, and she received the Lifetime Achievement Award in 1997 from the American Transit Association. Her awards from Civil Rights groups and African American publications are numerous.

What does Rosa Parks have in common with George Washington?

They have both received the Congressional Gold Medal, which is defined by Congress as the "highest expression of national appreciation for distinguished achievement and contributions." It's the highest honor that the United States government can give. Nelson Mandela received the medal in 1998, and Rosa Parks received hers in 1999.

AMERICAN VOICES

❝ People who have no position or money and have only the power of their courage and character are always there before the political leaders. . . . We must never, ever forget the power of ordinary people to stand in the fire for the cause of human dignity, and to touch the hearts of people that have almost turned to stone. ❞

—President **William Jefferson Clinton**, presenting Rosa Parks with the Congressional Gold Medal in June 1999

On February 4, 2003, Rosa Parks had her ninetieth birthday. Is she retired?

Although Rosa Parks retired from John Conyers's office in 1988, she has never wanted to stop working, learning, and teaching. While still in her eighties, she worked with her foundation, began Buddhist meditation, learned to use a computer and to swim, and collected recipes for a vegetarian cookbook. She has published three books: *Rosa Parks: My Story*, an autobiography for young adults; a collection of letters called *Dear Mrs. Parks: A Dialogue with Today's Youth*; and *Quiet Strength*, a book about the importance of religion in her life.

People have often asked Rosa Parks what still needs to be done. What does she answer?

She says that we must all still free our minds of racism and believe in freedom and justice for *all* people, of all races and all religions, everywhere in the world.

"We dare defend our rights" is the state motto of Alabama. It began as the motto of the segregationists and of the slave owners, who assumed that "we" meant only white men. But Rosa Parks was taught that "we" could be black people defending *their* rights. Rosa dares us to understand "we" as all people—all people, including children, defending what is right.

Rosa Parks says, "I want to be remembered as a person who stood up to injustice, who wanted a better world for young people; and most of all I want to be remembered as a person who wanted to be free. And my fight will continue as long as people are being oppressed."

February 4, 1913	Rosa McCauley born in Tuskegee, Alabama
1918	Begins school in Pine Level
1919	African American soldiers returning from World War I are met with violence
1924	Begins attending the Montgomery Industrial School for Negro Girls
1929	Leaves school to care for sick grandmother
March 1931	Nine African American young men arrested in Scottsboro, Alabama
December 1932	Marries Raymond Parks
1933	Graduates from high school
1941	Gets job at desegregated air-force base, Maxwell Field
1943	Joins the NAACP and becomes secretary of Montgomery branch; begins working as volunteer for E. D. Nixon
1945	Registers to vote
1949	Becomes adviser to the NAACP Youth Council
May 1954	United States Supreme Court decision in *Brown v. Board of Education* finds segregation in schools to be unconstitutional
Summer 1955	Attends workshop at Highlander Folk School; meets Septima Clark
August 1955	Meets Martin Luther King Jr.
December 1955	Arrested for refusing to give up seat on bus; Montgomery bus protest begins
January 1956	Loses job at Montgomery Fair department store

November 13, 1956	Supreme Court declares segregation on buses to be unconstitutional
December 21, 1956	Bus protest ends; Montgomery buses are integrated
1957	The Parks family moves to Detroit, Michigan
1963	March on Washington, D.C.
1964	Civil Rights Act of 1964 signed by President Lyndon Johnson
1965	Selma to Montgomery protest march; 1965 Voting Rights Act signed by President Johnson; Rosa Parks begins working for Congressman John Conyers
1977	Raymond Parks dies; Rosa's brother, Sylvester McCauley, dies
1979	Rosa Parks's mother dies
1980	First woman to receive Martin Luther King Jr. Nonviolent Peace Prize
1988	With Elaine Easton Steele, founds Rosa and Raymond Parks Institute for Self-Development; retires from working for John Conyers
1989	Attends dedication of Civil Rights Memorial in Montgomery
1992	Publishes first book, Rosa Parks: My Story, with Jim Haskins
1994	Goes to Stockholm, Sweden, to receive the Rosa Parks Peace Prize
June 6, 1999	Receives Congressional Gold Medal from President Clinton
December 1, 2000	Rosa Parks Library and Museum opened by Troy University, Montgomery
2005	Fiftieth anniversary of the beginning of the Montgomery bus boycott

SUGGESTED READING

NONFICTION

Friese, Kai. *Rosa Parks: The Movement Organizes*. Englewood Cliffs, NJ: Silver Burdett, 1990.

Hull, Mary. *Rosa Parks: Civil Rights Leader*. New York: Chelsea House, 1994.

King, Casey, and Linda Barrett Osborne. *Oh, Freedom!: Kids Talk about the Civil Rights Movement with the People Who Made It Happen*. New York: Alfred A. Knopf, 1997.

McKissack, Patricia, and Frederick McKissack. *The Civil Rights Movement in America from 1865 to the Present*. Chicago: Children's Press, 1987.

Parks, Rosa. *Dear Mrs. Parks*. New York: Lee and Low, 1996.

———. *My Story*. New York: Dial, 1992.

Rochelle, Belinda. *Witnesses to Freedom: Young People Who Fought for Civil Rights*. New York: Lodestar, 1993.

Siegel, Beatrice. *The Year They Walked: Rosa Parks and the Montgomery Bus Boycott*. New York: Simon & Schuster, 1992.

FICTION

Curtis, Christopher Paul. *The Watsons Go to Birmingham—1963*. New York: Delacorte, 1995.

Littlesugar, Amy. *Freedom School, Yes!* New York: Philomel, 2001.

Robinet, Harriette Gillem. *Walking to the Bus-Rider Blues*. New York: Atheneum, 2000.

Taylor, Mildred D. *Roll of Thunder, Hear My Cry*. New York: Dial, 1976.

SELECTED BIBLIOGRAPHY

Branch, Taylor. *Parting the Waters: America in the King Years, 1954–63.* New York: Simon & Schuster, 1988.

Brinkley, Douglas. *Rosa Parks.* New York: Viking Penguin, 2000.

Brown, Cynthia Stokes, ed. *Ready from Within: Septima Clark and the Civil Rights Movement.* Navarro, CA: Wild Trees Press, 1986.

Crawford, Vicki L., Jacqueline Anne Rouse, and Barbara Woods, eds. *Women in the Civil Rights Movement: Trailblazers and Torchbearers, 1941–1965.* Brooklyn, NY: Carlson, 1990.

Durr, Virginia. *Outside the Magic Circle.* Tuscaloosa: University of Alabama Press, 1985.

Garrow, David, ed. *The Walking City: The Montgomery Bus Boycott, 1955–1956.* Brooklyn, NY: Carlson, 1989.

Gray, Fred. *Bus Ride to Justice.* Montgomery, AL: Black Belt Press, 1995.

King, Martin Luther, Jr. *Stride Toward Freedom.* New York: Harper, 1958.

Olson, Lynne. *Freedom's Daughters: The Unsung Heroines of the Civil Rights Movement from 1830 to 1970.* New York: Scribner, 2001.

Parks, Rosa. *Quiet Strength.* Grand Rapids, MI: Zondervan, 1994.

Robinson, Jo Ann. *The Montgomery Bus Boycott and the Women Who Started It.* Knoxville: University of Tennessee Press, 1989.

Thornton, J. Mills, III. "Challenge and Response in the Montgomery Bus Boycott of 1955–1957." *Alabama Review*, vol. 33, 1980: pp. 163–235.

Washington, Booker T. *Up from Slavery.* New York: Doubleday, Page, 1901.

Williams, Juan. *Eyes on the Prize: America's Civil Rights Years 1954–1965.* New York: Viking Penguin, 1987.